BOLD

12 Character-Building Lessons

BIBLE KIDS

for Children's Ministry

Group

Loveland, Colorado

Bold Bible Kids

Credits

Contributors: Karl D. Bastian, Kathy Brand, Jules Erickson, Katie Garcia, Sheila Halasz, Debbie A. Neufeld, Ken Niles, Larry Shallenberger, Dave Thornton, Wendy L. Watros, Sharon Wilharm, Paul Woods

Editor: Lori Haynes Niles

Quality Control Editor: Dave Thornton

Chief Creative Officer: Joani Schultz

Copy Editor: Betty Taylor

Art Director: Ragont Design

Cover Art Director: Jeff A. Storm

Cover Designer: Becky Hawley

Computer Graphic Artist: Ragont Design

Cover Illustrator: Michael Morris

Illustrators: Mary Ragont and Van Severen Studios

Production Manager: Peggy Naylor

Library of Congress Cataloging-in-Publication Data

Bold Bible kids.
    p. cm.
  ISBN 0-7644-2114-X (alk. paper)
  1. Children in the Bible—Study and teaching. 2. Christian education of children. I. Group Publishing.
BS576.B65 1999
220.9'2'083—dc21
                                      98-40799
                                           CIP

10 9 8 7 6 5 4 3   08 07 06 05 04 03 02 01 00
Printed in the United States of America.

Visit our Web site: www.grouppublishing.com

Contents

Introduction

A rejected child crying in the desert. A humble slave girl in a leprous politician's home. An unnamed little boy with barley loaves to munch on. What made these young people's stories significant enough to become a permanent part of the record of God's loving plans for his people? And with so few verses devoted to most of those stories, how can we help those kids' stories reach into the lives of today's kids?

These are *Bold Bible Kids*. Kids who have crises and issues amazingly similar to those of the kids you teach each week. Kids who triumphed in the face of difficult circumstances. Kids who showed remarkable resiliency and enormous character under pressure.

We don't really know the ages of the children whose stories come to life in these pages. We have allowed the Scripture to define youth. Many were probably teenagers or very young adults as their stories began to be recorded. You'll meet each one as part of the unique culture he or she lived in. Your students will make toys inspired by Egyptian artifacts and wear crowns designed in the fashion of Greek champions. They'll think about what it might have been like to be a child slave or to grow up as a child of mixed ethnicity without a father figure, and they'll struggle with the intense pain of the biblical equivalent of a stepchild. You and your students will find out how these young people triumphed and enriched the lives of those around them to become enduring testimonies to God's faithfulness.

Each lesson provides an opportunity to travel through a different child's life, to experience what it might have been like to be right there, and to explore how each child's example might affect the way we live today. Like taking a walk with a friend, spending time with these *Bold Bible Kids* will be sure to change your kids.

Have an incredible journey!

A Boy Named "God Hears"

Kids Can pray to God when life gets difficult.

Your Kids and the Bible

Chances are, at least one child in your classroom will closely identify with Ishmael's life. Culturally, Ishmael was the ancient equivalent of a modern stepchild. Ishmael's mother was Sarah's servant, Hagar. Sarah was barren and struggled to believe that God would make good on his promise to make Abraham and Sarah parents of a burgeoning nation. In a faithless act, Sarah followed local custom and gave Hagar to Abraham as a surrogate. In spite of her role in orchestrating Ishmael's birth, Sarah developed an antagonistic relationship with Hagar. Shortly after Isaac's birth, she saw Ishmael mock her infant. Sarah felt that Ishmael was a threat to Isaac. She was filled by fear that somehow Ishmael, instead of her tiny son, Issac, might inherit Abraham's promise. She convinced Abraham to drive Ishmael and his mother away from the camp. Faced with certain death in the wilderness, Ishmael and Hagar experienced the meaning of Ishmael's name, "God Hears."

Certainly being a member of a blended family does not predetermine Ishmael's tragedies for any of your pupils. But unfortunately, the reality of blended and sometimes broken families can leave children feeling as Ishmael did: left out and unsure of their roles in their families. Ishmael's story can provide children with confidence that regardless of the conditions of their families, they are still valued by God and have important jobs to do for him. Every child in your class can discover that although young people occasionally face terrible hardships, God still hears and answers.

Simple Supplies

- index cards
- a clothesline
- a sheet
- a bright lamp
- a large bull's-eye target made from bright construction paper
- masking tape
- a coin
- plain white paper
- a video recorder (optional)
- a spring-type clothespin for each child

- crayons or markers
- craft sticks
- scissors
- glue
- photocopies of the "Tough Times Cards" (p. 11)
- photocopies of the crocodile head, tail, and feet (p. 12)
- photocopies of the "Boy Named 'God Hears'" handout (p. 10)

focus FUN

(5 to 10 minutes)

Before class, write the numbers "2" through "5" on individual index cards. Have one child be the dealer. Have the child choose the card from the top of the deck and call out the number written on the card. Tell children to quickly form "families" with the number of members called out. When they have formed each group, they are to call out, "No room in the family." Tell kids the object of the game is to be a part of the family. Play another round until each of the cards has been played. Ask:

- **If you were left out, how did it feel?**
- **Do you think it was fair that some people were left out of the families?**
- **Can you think of any fairy tales or stories in which a character didn't feel as if he or she was a welcome member of the family?**
- **How would you feel if you were to go home and find out that there was no longer any room for you?**

Say: **We're going to meet an older boy in the Bible who found out that there was no longer room for him in his family. Our feelings were only part of a game, but this boy named Ishmael really did lose his place in his family, even though he was there first.**

A Walk in Ishmael's Shoes
(15 minutes)

Say: **Ishmael's mother, Hagar, was a servant from the land of Egypt. Ishmael's father, Abraham, was from the land of Ur. Abraham later became known as the father of the Jewish nation. As Ishmael grew up, he probably experienced parts of both his father's and mother's worlds. We don't know what toys Ishmael played with as a child, but we do know that one toy many Egyptian children played with was a wooden crocodile with a wooden jaw. Let's make a similar toy now.**

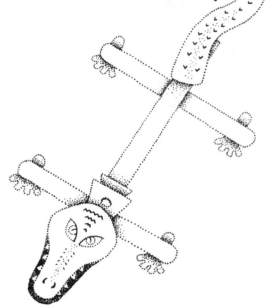

Give each student a clothespin and a photocopy of the crocodile head, feet, and tail (p. 12). Have kids each color a head, cut it out, and glue the headpiece to the top of the clothespin. Pass out the craft sticks. Have kids each fashion a crocodile torso by stacking three craft sticks on top of one another and gluing them together. Have them each make legs for their crocodiles by breaking two craft sticks in half, then gluing them perpendicularly to the torsos. Have them glue the clothespin heads to one end of the bodies, and tails to the other end. Have them each glue a paper foot to each leg. By squeezing the clothespins open, the jaws of the crocodiles will move.

(20 minutes)

A Leap into the Bible

Before class use a clothesline to hang a sheet across the room, or tack the sheet to the walls in a corner of the room. Set a bright lamp behind the sheet. Explain to the children that today's Bible story is found in Genesis 21. Tell the children that they are going to act out a shadow play. One of the children will be the narrator and read the story while the other children act out the story behind the sheet. Explain that the lamp will cast their shadows on the sheet for the audience to see. Let a couple of children demonstrate by going behind the sheet.

teacher TIP:

If you have a large class, assign a new set of actors and a new audience and have them perform the play a second time. If you have a smaller class, videotape and play back their performance on-screen so that students can be their own audience.

Assign the roles of narrator, Abraham, Sarah, Hagar, Ishmael, and the angel of God. Give the narrator the "Boy Named 'God Hears'" handout (p. 10). Have the narrator read the story from the handout while the actors pantomime the story.

After the shadow play, say: **It was not right for Ishmael to make fun of Isaac.** Ask:

● **Do you think the punishment Sarah gave Ishmael was fair?**

● **How do you think Ishmael felt when his father, Abraham, told him to leave the camp?**

Say: **Before Ishmael was born, God promised Hagar that her child would be the father of many nations.** Ask:

● **When she thought she might die in the desert, what do you think Hagar thought about the promise God had made to her?**

Say: **Ishmael cried out to God when his life was difficult. Today, kids can also cry out to God in prayer when life gets difficult. Let's play a game that shows how important it is to pray to God when you are going through hard times.**

teacher TIP:

If you are videotaping the play, it may be appropriate to let an older child operate the recorder with supervision. Make sure to test the video recorder, TV, and VCR to make sure you are able to record and play back the story; wasted minutes in a lesson can lead to discipline problems.

racing AHEAD

(10 to 15 minutes)

Before class, tape the bull's-eye to the wall. Make a tape line on the floor about five feet away from the target. Photocopy and cut apart the "Tough Times Cards" (p. 11). Stack them in a deck on the table. Give a sheet of paper to each child. Have children each make a paper airplane in any way they want to.

Say: **The Bible tells us that Ishmael became an expert archer. Let's pretend that we are archers and that these airplanes are our arrows. We are going to take turns trying to hit the bull's-eye. Hitting the bull's-eye can be like trusting God with our concerns during hard times.** Have children form a line. Ask the first child to pick up a Tough Times Card and read it aloud.

Say: **I'm going to have you flip a coin. If you get "heads," we are going to pretend you chose**

teacher TIP:

If you have nonreaders, pair them with readers or read the card aloud to them. Also, if you have a large group, consider setting up multiple stations so that each station includes eight or fewer kids.

to pray to God for help. If you get "tails," we are going to pretend you did not pray for help. Have each child flip the coin. If the child gets heads, have him or her make up a brief prayer to pray if he or she were really experiencing that particular hardship. Then tell the child to throw the "arrow" and try to hit the target. If the child gets tails, have that child think of a way someone might try to handle the situation without God's help. Tell the child to bend the nose of his or her airplane so the point is very crooked and then try to hit the bull's-eye. Keep playing until everybody has had a turn. Collect all the airplanes.

Ask:

● Which of the "arrows" had a better chance of hitting the bull's-eye?

● How is throwing a straight arrow at the target like praying to God when you are having a hard time?

● How is throwing a crooked arrow like trying to handle difficult circumstances without going to God for help?

Say: **Praying does not mean God will automatically take our problems away. But trying to handle difficult situations without God's help is like flying the seriously damaged paper plane. God promises to hear our prayer and give us help with our problems, in the same way he heard Ishmael's prayer. We can pray to God when life gets difficult.**

following the footsteps

(5 minutes)

Give each child a sheet of plain white paper and crayons or markers.

Say: **Ishmael's name meant "God hears." In the desert, Ishmael learned firsthand that God did hear his prayers. Every time Ishmael heard his name, he could remember the time God rescued him from a horrible situation, one of the hardest times of his life. Let's take a minute to think about a time God heard your prayers when you were in a particularly difficult situation.** Have children write about or draw their memories. Have the kids divide into groups of three and share what they wrote or drew on their papers.

Give the kids an opportunity to pray in their groups, thanking God for the ways he has answered their prayers.

Say: **When Ishmael was in the desert, he cried out to God, and God answered his prayers. God has heard our prayers during hard times, just as he heard Ishmael's. We can pray to God when life gets difficult. God will hear us when we call out to him.**

Have the kids take their papers home and put them in a place to remind them that God wants them to pray to him when they face difficulty.

It was a terrible mistake. Ishmael had made fun of his half brother, Isaac. He called Isaac names and made fun of Isaac. Isaac was only a baby, and Ishmael should have known better. But he was so frustrated. Ishmael grew up thinking that he would inherit all of his father Abraham's wealth when he died. Ishmael thought that he would take Abraham's place as head of many nations.

But when Isaac was born, Ishmael worried that Isaac might be Abraham's heir. Ishmael knew that many years ago God had promised Abraham and Sarah that their child would lead many nations. Abraham was Ishmael's father, but Sarah was his stepmother. Hagar was his mother. Ishmael realized that he would not be the next leader of the people now that Isaac was born.

That's why Ishmael was so angry. And instead of doing anything worse, he made fun of Isaac, just to make himself feel a little better. When Sarah saw Ishmael picking on her son, she was terribly angry with him. She had waited her whole life for this baby, and she wanted to make sure that Ishmael would never hurt him. If she allowed him to make fun of little Issac, what was to keep Ishmael from really hurting him?

Sarah went to Abraham and insisted that Abraham kick Ishmael and Hagar out of their camp. Sarah wanted them to live somewhere far away. Abraham was very upset that Sarah wanted him to do this to Ishmael and Hagar. But God told Abraham to listen to Sarah and do what she asked him to do. Abraham was sad, but he obeyed and trusted God. He gave Ishmael and Hagar some food and a canteen full of water and made them leave their family and everyone they knew.

Abraham did not know what would happen to Ishmael and Hagar, but God promised Abraham that he would take care of Ishmael.

Ishmael and Hagar quickly got lost in the desert. They walked in big circles but could not find their way out of the desert. They used up all of their food and water. If they did not find water soon, they would die under the hot sun. Ishmael was very weak from the hot sun. Hagar dragged him underneath a bush to shade him. Hagar then walked away from Ishmael because she could not bear to watch him die.

Ishmael lay under the bush and cried. The Bible doesn't tell us if he cried words or not, but it does say that God heard him there. An angel came to talk to Hagar. He told her that Ishmael would be the father of many nations. The angel showed Hagar a well full of water close by. Hagar ran to fill her canteen with water and brought Ishmael a drink. Ishmael and his mother found their way out of the desert with God's help.

From that day on, Ishmael must have understood the special meaning of his name, because Ishmael means "God hears."

Tough Times Cards

You have to study for a really hard math test. You don't know how you will ever be ready for it. Math is a tough subject for you. If you don't get a B, your dad says you'll be grounded until you bring your grades up.

Your grandmother is very sick. Your mom says she might get worse and die. You love Grandma very much and are very worried about her.

You want to go to summer camp with all of your friends. Dad says that money is tight right now and he does not know if you will be able to go. You don't want to be the only kid stuck at home this summer.

You broke your leg and have to wear a cast for two months. You have a newspaper route, but you can't ride your bike. Your parents both work long hours and can't help you. You don't want to lose your job.

Your parents have been fighting a lot lately. Jimmy's parents just got divorced. Your parents say they will always be together, but sometimes you get worried.

You just moved to a new city. Your new school is *huge*. The other students already have all the friends they need. You are not sure if you are going to fit in. The only kids who will play with you are some rough kids who seem to get into a lot of trouble.

You have a piano recital in three weeks. You get very nervous when you play the piano in front of other people. You made many mistakes the last time and totally embarrassed yourself. You just *can't* get up in front of people again.

Your baseball team practices all the time. You are getting tired of always going to practice. You never have time to do what you want. You'd like to quit, but your parents say you have to finish what you've started. You have two long months left.

Miriam: Bold Action for God

Kids Can take bold action for what is right.

Your Kids and the Bible

Boldness and initiative seem to be born into some children. As babies, they seem to know what they want and are not afraid to demand it. These children *allow* their parents to live in *their* houses. When children like these learn right from wrong, they have no problem standing up and being bold for what is right. However, these abilities do not come naturally or easily to all children. Many children are intimidated by their bolder peers and even think of them as rude or bossy. Some children in your class will never be domineering leaders, and that's OK. Your job is *not* to make a classroom full of leaders. Your job is to help children realize that it's all right for kids to take bold action for what is right. Kids don't have to take bold action all the time, but they need to know God will help them to take bold action if it is for the right cause.

Miriam was a girl who took bold initiative at an early age. She was Moses' older sister, born into a Hebrew family at a time when the Egyptian Pharaoh was afraid of the growing Hebrew population. The Egyptians used the Hebrews as slaves. To ensure a strong Egyptian rule, the Pharaoh ordered all Hebrew baby boys to be killed. Miriam could not stand the thought of losing Moses, who had been spared by the midwives. She knew she had to take bold action for what was right. She had to go against the Pharaoh's horrible plan. She and her mother put baby Moses in a handmade basket and sent him down the Nile River to save him from death. Miriam secretly waited in the tall grass to make sure her brother would be safe. While at the river, the Pharaoh's daughter found Moses, and she wanted to keep the baby. After Miriam cleverly suggested her own mother be allowed to nurse the baby until he was weaned, the Pharaoh's daughter took Moses to live with her and the Pharaoh (Exodus 2:1-9). It is believed that Moses lived in the palace as an infant but was taken care of by his own loving Hebrew mother.

Miriam must have been sad that her brother would not be allowed to play the Hebrew games she loved, nor would he be raised in a home where God was an integral member of the family. However, Miriam knew that killing is against God's will, and she had to take bold action for what was right. She continued her boldness as she became Scripture's first prophetess (Exodus 15:20). Miriam also led the Israelite women in a victory song and celebration following the destruction of Pharaoh's army at the Red Sea (Exodus 15:20-22). We learn from her that with God's help, even young children can take bold action for what is right and that bold children can become groundbreaking adults.

Simple Supplies

- **enough cotton balls for half the class**
- **a bag or basket containing the following items: one nonbreakable cup, a baby rattle or baby toy, a radish, one scarf, grass or cut-up pieces of green paper placed into plastic bags or secured with rubber bands (one item per child)**
- **two bags of differently colored beans, such as one bag of kidney beans and one bag of pinto beans**
- **(three beans per child)**
- **photocopies of the game board (p. 21) or blank paper**
- **enough radishes for everyone to have one (If radishes are not easily available, you may use peeled potatoes.)**
- **plastic knives for everyone**
- **toothpicks**
- **pencils and paper**

(10 minutes)

focus FUN

Have children form pairs. If there's an uneven number of children, one group may have three. The older person will be a mom or dad, and the younger person will be a son or daughter. Invite all the "parents" to take a cotton ball.

Say: **The parents here today love their children very much, and they are bringing home a pet for the family. Raise your hand if you have ever been to a pet store. The first thing I want you to do with your partner is choose a name for your pet.** Allow pairs a couple of minutes to choose a name. **Now I want you to play with your pet. You might want to teach it to roll over, or play Hide-and-Seek with it.** Pause. **Baby pets get tired easily. Find a good place for your pet to sleep.** Allow time for kids to put their pets to sleep. **Tell your family member one thing you would like to do with your pet when it gets bigger.** Wait until partners have shared an answer. **Wait, I just got a letter for this class.** Pretend to open a letter and read.

"**Dear families, I am writing this to you from my office downtown. I have some bad news for some of you. Families in this room who have sons or daughters must give up any pets they own. Some families in another part of town do not have children. They may keep their pets. However, all of your pets must be destroyed. Sincerely, Your Leader.**"

Say: **Remember, you really love your new pet, and you don't want it destroyed. What could your family do?** Let the children discuss their options for a while, and then ask pairs to share their suggestions. Ask:

● **How did you feel when you first got to play with your pet?**

● **How did you feel when I told you that you would have to give up your pet?**

● **What kind of real situations have you been in when you had to think quickly to prevent something bad from happening?** If no one has anything to add, tell students that even though they can't think of anything right now, by the time they go home, they'll each have an answer to that question.

Say: **A girl in the Bible named Miriam had to solve an even more serious problem. Instead of saving a pet, she had to find a way to save her baby brother. She had to take bold action for what was right.**

(15 to 20 minutes)

A Leap into the Bible

Have the children sit on the floor and face the front of the room. Pass around a bag or a basket with a nonbreakable cup, a baby rattle or toy, a radish, one scarf, grass or cut-up pieces of green paper placed into baggies or secured with rubber bands.

As you read the story and you see the word "pause," allow or prompt the children to do the actions described in the story.

Say: **In the book of Exodus, chapter 2, verses 1 through 9, there is a story about a mother. Will the person with the scarf please put it on your head and come stand by me?** Pause. **Mothers in Bible times often wore coverings on their heads when they were outside. This mother had a bold and smart daughter named Miriam. Will the person with a radish please come stand by the mother?** Pause.

teacher TIP:

Make sure four children each pick one of the first four items. Everyone else will get the grass.

Miriam lived by the Nile River where many radishes were easily grown. Miriam's mother had a baby named Moses. **Will the person holding a rattle please come stand by Miriam?** Pause.

This family loved Moses very much. He could make the cutest faces to make Miriam happy. **Baby Moses, can you please show us one of your cute, silly faces?** Pause.

The Egyptian Pharaoh at that time did not want Hebrew people to get too powerful. The Egyptians used all the Hebrew people as slaves, and Pharaoh did not want to lose power over his slaves. He was so mean that he ordered all Hebrew baby boys to be killed so they wouldn't grow up and try to take over his government. **Let me see everyone's meanest Pharaoh face.** Pause.

Miriam and her mother were very scared. **Miriam and Mother, show us how scared you are because you know Pharaoh wants to kill baby Moses.** Pause.

They knew they had to come up with a plan to save Moses. They went down to the Nile River where the grass grew. **Will the people with grass please come up and kneel in a row in front of Miriam, Moses, and their mother?** Pause. We will pretend the river is in front of you. The grass was tall and waved gently in the wind. **Let's see how our grass can wave in the wind.** Pause.

Miriam and her mother chose some pieces of grass and wove them into a basket for Moses. Instruct Miriam and the mother to pick five people and help them form some kind of basket shape to hold Moses. If the class is small, the basket can be made with only two or three children. If your class is smaller than eight, it's OK if you use all the children to make the basket.

Miriam and her mother painted black tar on the grass to make it waterproof. **Let's see how you can paint the basket.** Pause. **Miriam put the baby in the basket and set it in the river.** Pause. **The Pharaoh's daughter was at the river. Will the person with a cup please come and scoop water at the end of all the grass?** Pause. **After Moses was put in the basket, Miriam quickly went down near the Pharaoh's daughter and waited for the basket to float by.** Instruct the basket with Moses to slowly come down the river while the grass gently sways.

The Pharaoh's daughter was very excited to find a baby, but she knew she could not take care of a crying infant by herself. Miriam was right there to suggest a Hebrew lady who could take care of the baby until he grew older. **Miriam quickly went to get her own mother.** Pause. **Miriam's mother and Miriam quickly appeared and comforted the crying baby.** Pause. **Miriam and her mother were sad to let Moses go live with the Pharaoh's daughter** (pause), **but they were happy that Moses would be cared for by his own mother until he was old enough to eat solid food.** Pause. **They were thrilled that Moses would be saved from death.** Pause. **The** grass gave a final wave as the baby went off to start his new life. Pause.

Thank all of your participants, ask them to be seated, and ask:

● **How do you think Miriam felt when she saw the Pharaoh's daughter pick up her baby brother?**

● **How do you think Miriam and Moses' mother felt letting a cruel Egyptian family raise Moses instead of letting him stay in a loving Hebrew home?**

● **What might have been some of their concerns?**

● **Can you think of any other things that Miriam and her mother could have done to save Moses?**

● **What would have happened to Moses if his sister had not been bold enough to do what was right?**

● **What are some situations today that might require a child to stand up and take bold action for what is right?**

Say: **Miriam's story helps us to see that kids can overcome fear and take bold action for what is right when they need to. Let's find out more about Miriam's life.**

A Walk in Miriam's Shoes
(10 to 20 minutes)

Say: **Miriam lived in Egypt near the Nile River. Archaeologists tell us that Hebrew children at that time liked playing a game called Nine Holes. It is similar to the game we call Tick-Tack-Toe. Children drew the game board in the sand, or they carved it in stone. One interesting thing about this game is that only working people played this game. There is no record that any of the people in the palace played this, probably because they considered it too common. We know this because when archaeologists have studied the ancient Egyptian ruins, they have never found the game buried with royalty. They've found other games, but not this one. This one was found only in areas people worked, such as on the tops of pyramids.**

Miriam probably would not have played this game with her younger brother. Moses would not have known about it since he was living in the palace. Today we are going to use a game board on paper. The Egyptians made paper out of the same grass along the Nile River used to make Moses' basket. The paper was called papyrus. It was probably very expensive, so slaves wouldn't have used it.

To help us remember Miriam's story as we play, we are also going to write some words on our game board, even though Miriam's game board wouldn't have had any words.

Give children copies of the blank game board (p. 21), or have them draw their own. Then pass out pencils, and have children fill in the words as shown.

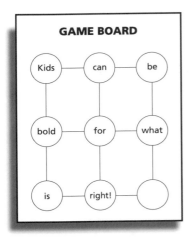

GAME BOARD

Kids — can — be

bold — for — what

is — right!

Say: **Find a partner who is at least two years older or younger than you. The youngest kids in the pairs will choose either their own game boards or their partners' to play with.** (Kids can be the same age if you don't have a combined-age group. Only one game board is needed for each pair.)

Give each pair three beans of each color, one color for each person. Say: **Take turns putting a bean on any circle on the game board. The first person to get three in a row, across or up and down, is the winner. When a player uses all three beans, he or she may move any of his or her beans to an open space. Keep playing until someone wins. The winner may shout, "Take bold action for what is right!" You can play until I say, "Take bold action for what is right!" and if your game isn't over, it will be a tie. When you go home today, you will be able to take this game with you. Play it with your family or friends to help them understand a little about Miriam's world and to know that kids can take bold action for what is right.**

teacher TIP:

This game can also be played outdoors if the weather and area are appropriate. Let children each pick three stones for their marking pieces instead of beans. If you have a sandy area or an area of dirt, let the children draw their own game boards with a stick. This would be really authentic. For a modern outdoor version, you could use chalk on a sidewalk or driveway. Make sure you send the paper game home as a visual reminder of the lesson's point.

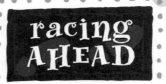

racing AHEAD

(15 minutes)

Say: **Remember the vegetable we said grew near the Nile River when Miriam was a little girl? It was a radish. Radishes were a very common food in Egypt, but they are different from most other vegetables.** Show the children a radish, and let them talk about the differences they see. Cut one open, and continue to look at it. Say: **Later, you'll get to taste a radish if you'd like to find out how unique they taste!**

Besides the Nine Hole game we already played, many of the people in Miriam's day played with dice. The richer people played with fancy dice made out of bones, but children from working families made dice out of anything they could find. They wanted to have fun just as the rich Egyptians did. I don't know if anyone ever made dice out of a radish, but we are going to try today.

Give each child a radish, a plastic knife, and a toothpick. Make a sample die as you show children how to cut the radish into the shape of a cube. It's OK if some of the red remains on the radish. Next show the children how they can make holes with their toothpicks on each of their radishes so they resemble dice. You might want to have several real dice available for the children to look at. Also, it would be helpful to have a large illustration of the dice markings on a chalkboard or piece of paper, similar to this:

As the children mark their dice, encourage them to taste a piece of their radish peelings. Talk about how radishes have a very strong taste. They are a very bold-tasting vegetable. Ask the children if they think Miriam liked to eat radishes when she was their age.

Say: **Now that we have made our dice, let's see if they work.**

Give children a blank piece of paper, and have them stand in circles of eleven or fewer people. You will need one pencil to pass around each circle. Going around each circle, have the first child write "2," the second child write "3," and so on until everyone has written a number. Older children may help younger children who are unsure of how to write their numbers. If there are fewer than eleven children, let some children hold two numbers. If there are more than eleven, form two circles. Have the person holding the number 2 step into the middle of the circle and roll his or her die along with the sample die from the teacher. The number of the two dice added together will identify one person. The person throwing the dice will add the numbers and say to the person identified by the number, "Quickly now, before you're old, tell how you know someone's bold." The person whose number was rolled will then finish the sentence "I'd know someone was bold for what is right if…"

The person in the center will then pass the teacher's die to the answering person, making sure to keep his or her own die. Have the answering person give his or her number to someone else to hold and take the place of the person in the center. This will ensure that everyone gets a turn. When everyone has had a turn, say: **You really thought of a lot of ways your friends could take bold action for what is right. You can take your homemade die home with you to use with a game that needs dice. If you let your die lay out in the air for a few days, it will get as hard as a rock.**

Sometimes the radishes dry so that you can still see the dots, and sometimes they dry and shrivel up right where

If your class members are young or you have kids who struggle with addition, point to each dot on the dice and let the kids count out the total together.

the dots are. Come back next week, and tell me how your die looked after a week. No matter how they dry, remember that radishes are unique, bold-tasting vegetables that grew in ancient Egypt, and you can be kids who take bold action for what is right.

following the footsteps

(12 to 15 minutes)

Say: **Miriam was very bold as a child, and she continued to take bold action when she grew up. She went on to become the first woman recorded to have said things inspired by God. She was called a prophetess. She also was with Moses when he parted the Red Sea. Miriam led the Israelite women in a victory song and celebration after the Pharaoh's army drowned in the Red Sea. God used her in a big way all through her life.**

Instruct children to form groups of no more than four. Say: **I would like you to pretend that you are all grown up. Try to think of some ways you could show your boldness to stand up for what is right as an adult.**

Let children discuss this in their groups without sharing with the class as a whole.

Say: **Now I want you to think about one way you thought adults could take bold action for what is right. Take a few minutes in your group to discuss how you, today as a kid, could try to take bold action for the same thing. I want the oldest person in the group to write one way that your group could take bold action for what is right this week.** Let the children record their thoughts on paper.

When children have finished writing one example, ask:

● **Which was easier to think of an example for: a child or an adult? Why?**

● **Tell me how it is different for a child to be bold than it is for an adult?**

Say: **Sometimes we may think that adults have an easier time being bold for what is right, but kids can be just as bold because God promises to give us courage as we try to do what is right.**

After the groups discuss their answers, pray: **Dear Lord, please be with our class as we...**(finish with the answers the children recorded). **Help us to remember that we really can take bold action for what is right. Help us all to take action on what you lead us to believe is right. Amen.**

GAME BOARD

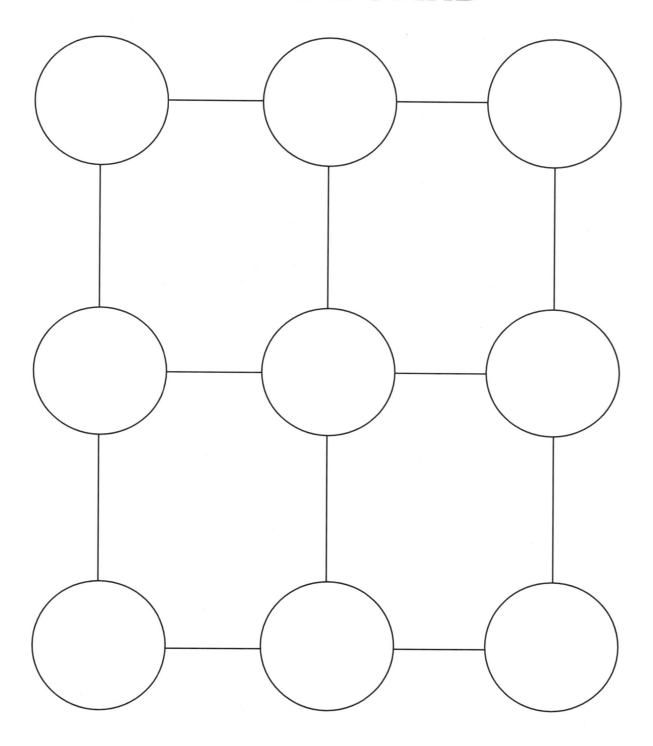

Samuel Heard a Voice and Made a Choice!

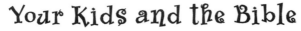

Kids Can hear and respond to God's voice.

Your Kids and the Bible

Samuel was a very special boy. The answer to a desperate prayer of a barren mother, Samuel was dedicated to the Lord and given by his mother to serve in the tabernacle of Israel. While many of the children in your class were direct answers to prayer, *all* are gifts from God and can live lives dedicated to serving him.

Children are used to being told what to do. Parents, teachers, and other adults give them instructions every day. When it comes to their relationships with God, kids need to know they can each have a *personal* relationship with the Lord. A child's relationship with God does not have to come through an adult. God is not just someone who adults talk about and teach children about. God is someone who wants to talk to them directly, and he wants them to respond directly to him!

Samuel was a young child when he first heard the voice of the Lord. Interestingly enough, we learn in I Samuel 3:7 (*after* the story of hearing God's voice) that "Samuel did not yet know the Lord." God spoke to Samuel *before* he had a relationship with him! What wonderful confirmation that God is reaching out to *all* the kids in your class, both those who have chosen to have a personal relationship with him and those who may not know him yet. Your job as a teacher is not to tell children what God is saying, but to teach them to listen for God's voice and to know how to respond.

In this lesson your children will learn about Samuel's life in the tabernacle and how he learned to listen and respond to God's voice. Samuel wore an ephod just as the adult priests did, demonstrating that he was ready to serve the God of Israel even as a boy. Through the different activities, your children will focus on *listening* to God and responding. Then, like Samuel, when they hear God's voice, they will be able to make the right choice—to listen and obey.

Simple Supplies

- two plastic cups
- a string (at least five feet long but may be up to twenty feet, depending on the quality of the string)
- felt squares (gold, blue, and purple are best)
- red yarn
- glue
- a stapler
- jewels (giant plastic sequins or paper cutouts)
- index cards or slips of paper
- pencils or pens

focus FUN

(10 minutes)

Before class, poke a small hole in the center of the bottom of two plastic cups. Put the ends of a length of string through the holes in the cups, and tie each end in a knot so that the string can't be pulled back through the hole. To hear through the "phone," the string must be taut. You will speak into one cup. The sound waves will travel down the cup, converge at the knot, travel all the way along the string until they hit the other knot, and then be amplified by the other cup. In this way, the person listening through that cup will be able to hear your message.

Say: **I am going to tell each of you a different secret message. Don't tell anyone what you hear. After everyone has had a turn, you will be able to tell what *your* secret message was.** As each child takes the cup, ask: **Do you hear me?** After the child answers "yes" through the telephone, say through the telephone: **Your secret message is...** and say the child's name. After every child has had a chance to hear his or her "secret message," say: **On the count of three, I want you all to say out loud what *your* secret message was. Ready? One, two, three...** Kids will all say their names.

Wow! They all sounded so different! Ask:
- **What was different about each person's message?**
- **In what way were they all the same?**

Say: **Just as I had a message for you, God has a message for each of us! God's call to each of us is different because we are all different. But God asks each of us to answer and obey the message he has for us.**

God called out to a boy in the Bible in much the same way I called out to you. Of course, God didn't need a device like the one we used. Samuel was just a young child—maybe eight or nine when this story happened. But when he heard God's voice, he made a choice to listen and obey. We

can hear and answer God's voice too.

A Walk in Samuel's Shoes
(20 minutes)

Say: **Samuel was a very special boy. In fact, it was a miracle that he was even born! Samuel's mother, Hannah, was unable to have children, so she prayed and asked God to give her a son. She promised that if God answered her prayers, she would give her son to the Lord to serve in the tabernacle. God answered her prayer, so she kept her promise, even though it must have been terribly hard to allow her precious son to live away from her. That is why, unlike other Israelite kids, Samuel lived in the tabernacle and served with the priests. The Bible says that Samuel wore an ephod as the priests did, even though he was only a boy. An ephod was a very special piece of clothing that only those who worked in the house of God could wear. The way these garments were made is described in detail in the Bible. If you saw a person with an ephod on, you knew he was serving the Lord. Let's look up some verses in the Bible that describe what ephods looked like.**

Choose children to look up these verses and read them to the class.

● Exodus 28:6—"Make the ephod of gold, and of blue, purple and scarlet yarn, and of finely twisted linen—the work of a skilled craftsman."

● Exodus 35:9—"…onyx stones and other gems to be mounted on the ephod and breastpiece."

Say: **Our ephods won't look exactly like the ones the priests wore, but they will be close enough to remind us that we are servants of God, too, even though we don't live in the tabernacle or work with priests.**

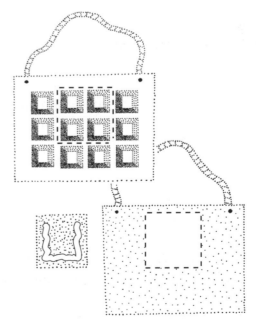

Give each child one felt square for an ephod plus another one-fourth square for a "secret" pocket on the back of the ephod, twelve jewel-like stones, an eighteen-inch piece of red yarn to hang the ephod around the child's neck, and some glue.

Show the children how to glue the jewels in three rows with four gems in each row. Then have them turn the ephods over, and show them how to put glue around the edges of three sides of the smaller pieces of felt. Show them how to place the pocket with the unglued edge at the top. Have children staple the yarn to the upper corners of the breast-plates so they can wear the ephods.

Have the children put on their ephods. Say: **Now you look as if you might be a child working in the tabernacle. You will find out what the secret pocket is for later in our lesson.** Ask:

● **How do you think Samuel felt when he put on his ephod?**

● **When do you think it might have been difficult to be known as the boy who wore the ephod?**

● **What do you think the benefits of living with the priests at the tabernacle might have been?**

● **How do you feel when you think of yourself as a servant of God?**

Say: **All servants have to be especially good at one thing. They have to know how to listen and respond to the voice of the one they serve. Samuel became very good at that, and we're going to find out how.**

"They fashioned the breastpiece—the work of a skilled craftsman. They made it like the ephod: of gold, and of blue, purple and scarlet yarn, and of finely twisted linen. It was square—a span long and a span wide—and folded double. Then they mounted four rows of precious stones on it. In the first row there was a ruby, a topaz and a beryl; in the second row a turquoise, a sapphire and an emerald; in the third row a jacinth, an agate and an amethyst; in the fourth row a chrysolite, an onyx and a jasper. They were mounted in gold filigree settings. There were twelve stones, one for each of the names of the sons of Israel, each engraved like a seal with the name of one of the twelve tribes" (Exodus 39:8-14).

(15 minutes)

A Leap into the Bible

Give each child a piece of paper, and ask each to tear the paper into four pieces. Have children write their names on each piece. Have them fold the papers and give them back to you. Ask all the children to lie down on their backs as though they are sleeping. As they "sleep," draw a child's name from the pile, and put it aside. Tell the children that when they hear their names, they are to come to you and say, "Here I am; you called me."

As each child comes to you, say, "I did not call; go back and lie down." Do this until every child's name has been called.

After a name has been drawn three times, say, "Go and lie down, and if he calls you, say, 'Speak, Lord, for your servant is listening.' " Children may need to be coached on their lines.

Then say: **What we have just done is a lot like what happened to a young boy in the Bible.** Open your Bible to 1 Samuel 3:1-11. Paraphrase or read the passage directly from your Bible, or use the version following. To help them connect the experience to the story, ask children to raise their hands when they hear something that happened to Samuel that was similar to something they just experienced.

Ask:
- **Why do you think Samuel thought it was Eli who called him?**
- **Who do you think God might use in your life to help you hear his voice?**
- **What are other ways we can hear God speaking to us?**
- **What does it feel like when you hear God's words?**

1 Samuel 3:1-11

The boy Samuel ministered before the Lord under Eli. In those days the word of the Lord was rare; there were not many visions.

One night Eli, whose eyes were becoming so weak that he could barely see, was lying down in his usual place. The lamp of God had not yet gone out, and Samuel was lying down in the temple of the Lord, where the ark of God was. Then the Lord called Samuel.

Samuel answered, "Here I am." And he ran to Eli and said, "Here I am; you called me."

But Eli said, "I did not call; go back and lie down." So he went and lay down.

Again the Lord called, "Samuel!" And Samuel got up and went to Eli and said, "Here I am; you called me."

"My son," Eli said, "I did not call; go back and lie down."

Now Samuel did not yet know the Lord: The word of the Lord had not yet been revealed to him.

The Lord called Samuel a third time, and Samuel got up and went to Eli and said, "Here I am; you called me."

Then Eli realized that the Lord was calling the boy. So Eli told Samuel, "Go and lie down, and if he calls you, say, 'Speak, Lord, for your servant is listening.' "So Samuel went and lay down in his place.

The Lord came and stood there, calling as at the other times, "Samuel! Samuel!"

Then Samuel said, "Speak, for your servant is listening."

And the Lord said to Samuel: "See, I am about to do something in Israel that will make the ears of everyone who hears of it tingle."

- **What are some ways we can respond when we hear God's words to us?**

Say: **Samuel heard and responded to God's voice. Even though we may not hear God speak to us with our ears, we can hear and respond to God's words, too.**

(10 minutes)

Have kids stand up. Say: **I want you to play along with me by listening and responding. As soon as you don't want to respond, please be seated. If your interest picks up, stand up again.**

Tell this "knock-knock" joke to the group.

Knock, knock.

Kids will ask, "Who's there?"

Banana.

Kids will ask, "Banana who?"

Now instead of finishing the joke as usual, just repeat those lines three times exactly as you did the first time, without explanation. Then say:

Knock, knock.

Kids will ask, "Who's there?"

Plum.

Kids will ask, "Plum who?"

Plumb sick of this banana and orange joke!

Most of the children will know this joke with the punch line being "Orange you glad I didn't say banana?" If they don't get it, tell the joke with the orange punch line; then retell the joke with the plumb punch line to illustrate your point. Ask:

● **How did you feel when I started to tell this joke you've heard again and again?**

● **How did you feel by about the third time I said "banana"?**

● **What's the purpose of responding even when you don't want to?**

● **What if you had stopped answering me?**

● **Have you ever gone to Sunday school or church and felt a little as you did when I was telling the knock-knock joke? How were the experiences similar?**

Say: **Samuel might have felt frustrated when God called him again and again while he was trying to go to sleep. You or I sure might have! But if Samuel felt that way, he didn't allow himself to act on those feelings. He answered every time, even though he didn't "get it" at first. We need to be like Samuel. We need to respond every time, even if we think we've heard the message before. If we stop listening because we get tired of hearing God's message or we don't see the point of answering, we can miss what God is trying to say to us. Sometimes God's message to us is repeated again and again until we *really* understand what he is saying.**

If your group members are young, you may wish to skip the questions related to church experience. However, this can be a powerful insight-provoking experience for older elementary kids who sometimes complain of having heard it all before.

Think of a message you've heard again and again. How can you respond better the next time you hear it?

(5 minutes)

Give each student a small index card and pen or pencil. Have children sit in a semicircle on the floor.

Say: **Samuel heard God's voice and made a choice to listen and obey. God is speaking to each one of us as well. Sometimes God speaks in a small voice that we almost hear, but most of the time God speaks through the Bible and through leaders in our lives such as parents, teachers, and pastors.**

Most of us know of things God has told us to do—but not all of us are listening and obeying. Sometimes we are too busy to listen; other times we have heard but not obeyed. Let's take some time right now to stop being busy and listen to God.

Ask the kids to close their eyes, bow their heads, and relax. Ask them to listen with their hearts and to each think of one thing that they know God has asked them to do. It may be something God told them through their parents, a teacher, or a pastor. It may be to obey their parents and clean their rooms; it may be to share Jesus with a friend at school; it may be to spend time each day reading the Bible and in prayer with God. Encourage each child to think of just one thing he or she knows God wants him or her to do. You can offer some suggestions to get them thinking, but challenge them to think of something personal.

After a few minutes, have them write what they thought of on their index cards. No one is to look at what others write—this is just between God and each student. Explain that not even the teacher will read their cards. (You may want to have them write the same thing on two cards and then collect one card without a name on it from each child so that the leaders can pray for them.)

Have each child fold the card and put it in the secret pocket on his or her ephod.

After everyone has finished, pray a prayer similar to this: **Dear God, today we have heard your voice, and we want to respond to you, to listen and obey as Samuel did. Please help us to not be so busy that we cannot hear you, and when we *do* hear you, give us a desire to obey. In Jesus' name, amen.**

David: The Responsible Shepherd

Kids Can be responsible with God's help.

Your Kids and the Bible

Responsible shepherding contributed to the welfare of Old Testament society. The people depended on sheep for wool, milk, and meat. Without the shepherd's constant guidance and management, sheep would die from animal attacks, eating poisonous vegetation, or falling off a cliff's edge. Because they have little ability to protect themselves, the sheep's welfare depended solely upon the quality of care they received from their shepherd.

Young David proved himself to be a responsible shepherd who was concerned with pleasing God as well as people. With the Lord's help, David risked his life to protect his sheep. He killed a lion and a bear when they threatened his flock. David also developed other skills that depended on responsible commitment, such as playing the harp. Upon his servants' recommendation, King Saul invited David to play for him. David and his harp-playing pleased Saul so much that he continued to request his playing and appointed David to be his armorbearer.

A society thrives when people live up to their responsibilities. Families function more peacefully, students learn more from what they're taught, businesses are more productive, and government more often makes decisions based on the good of the people than for personal gain.

Children will benefit from studying how David's boyhood responsibilities helped prepare him to lead Israel into days of glory. It's hard for kids to see how feeding the dog every day relates to their future success. Learning how David's responsibility and the trust it earned benefited both him and his kingdom can be a powerful source of encouragement to your kids.

Simple Supplies

- paper plates, marshmallows, marshmallow cream, paper towels, large craft sticks, and raisins
- markers or crayons
- blindfolds
- a cane or a thick stick
- rubber bands and an empty tissue box

- a robe
- sandals
- rocks
- photocopies of the "Shepherd Duties" story (p. 35)
- a heating source (oven, toaster oven, or electric skillet)
- a cookie sheet

focus FUN

(5 to 10 minutes)

Before class, for each child prepare a paper plate containing a handful of marshmallows, about five raisins (or more to eat while working), one large craft stick, and a small glob of marshmallow cream. Set out markers or crayons for each child.

Say: **Today we're learning about David, a young shepherd boy from the Bible. Being a shepherd was a big responsibility for David. Because sheep aren't too bright, they easily fall into dangerous situations. So David had to watch over his sheep all day, protecting them from wild animal attacks, from falling off cliffs, from eating poisonous things, and from getting lost. David didn't have a lot of free time to play games with his friends. In the summertime, when the hot sun turned the grass brown, David had to travel far from home to lead his sheep to greener pastures. He even had to sleep outside with his sheep while they were away from home.** Ask:

● **David had some difficult shepherding responsibilities, but what part of the job do you think was fun for David?**

Say: **Because David often had to call his sheep to follow him, he named each of his sheep. I bet David enjoyed thinking up different names for his sheep. Right now, each of you will create a marshmallow sheep and name it. You will get a plate full of sheep-making supplies. There's no right or wrong way to make your sheep. Construct your sheep however you wish, using the supplies on your plate. Then write the name you choose on the paper plate beside the finished project. We'll share the names of our flock and our reasons for choosing their names. After sharing your artwork with us, you may eat your sheep or save it to take home**

with you. Have older children help younger students. Pass out plates, or have a few kids at a time come for their supplies. Kids may need to wash sticky fingers after this activity.

After the kids have finished their creations, ask:

- **What is your sheep's name?**
- **Why did you choose that name?**

Say: **In Bible times, many children's names had special meanings. Do you have any ideas about what David's name might have meant?**

David's name meant "beloved." As we learn more about him, you may develop some ideas about why David was beloved. We'll also learn how David's responsibility with sheep led him into some even more important opportunities.

A Walk in David's Shoes
(15 minutes)

You'll need blindfolds for half the class.

Say: **Sheep respond only to their shepherd's voice. They get lost very easily if left to themselves, because they just go wherever the green grass leads. When David shouted a wandering or lost sheep's name, the sheep would follow his voice and return to the flock. Sheep won't follow a stranger's call, only their own shepherd's. We're going to play a game called "Lost Sheep." Half of you will be blindfolded lost Sheep, and half of you will be Shepherds. When I say "go," find a partner who's at least one year younger or older than you, and together decide who will play the blindfolded Sheep and who will play the calling Shepherd. When I call out, "Sheep!" stop talking and look at me. Go!** Allow one minute for children to form pairs (become the partner of anyone left without one); then point to the blindfolds and say: **Sheep!** Pause for their attention. **Now, Shepherds, come get blindfolds, and help your Sheep put them on if they want help.** Allow time for children to put on the blindfolds, and then say: **Sheep!** Pause. **Please tell your Shepherd what name you called your marshmallow sheep. This will be your name during the game. Shepherds, quietly practice calling your Sheep's name so your Sheep will get used to your voice. You have thirty seconds.**

Then say: **Sheep!** Pause. **When I say "Baa," Shepherds, guide your blindfolded Sheep to the middle of the room, gently spin them around three times, and then leave your Sheep there. Go stand against a wall, and wait for instructions. Sheep, you must stay put until you hear your Shepherd's voice. Any questions?** Answer any questions; then give the cue.

When all the Shepherds are standing at the wall, say: **When I clap my hands, Shepherds will call their sheep's names. Sheep, get on your hands and knees, and go find your shepherd.** (In a small room, Shepherds should use a whisper or soft voice.) **Sheep, crawl until you are able to touch your Shepherd; then you may remove your blindfold. Get ready.** Clap your hands. Encourage kids as they search out their Shepherds.

When all the Sheep have found their Shepherds, ask:

● **What might have happened if the Shepherds in our game had fallen asleep or hadn't cared enough to call out their Sheep's names?**

● **What might have happened to a lost sheep if David hadn't bothered to go find it?**

● **What might have happened to David if he had failed in his responsibility to go find a lost sheep?**

● **How is finding a lost sheep similar to one of your responsibilities?**

● **What happens when you don't take care of one of these responsibilities we just mentioned?**

● **What happens to you when you're faithful to your responsibilities?**

Say: **When we're faithful to our smaller responsibilities in life, God, our parents, and others learn that they can trust us with bigger, more important jobs. Kids can be responsible with God's help. David certainly found that out!**

(15 minutes)

A Leap into the Bible

Choose three older children to act out the following parts: David, a lion, and a bear. David will need a robe, sandals, a harp (one may be made by stretching rubber bands around an empty tissue box), and a staff (a cane or a thick stick). Provide David, the lion, and the bear with a photocopy of the "Shepherd Duties" story (p. 35) to read in preparation. They should remain out of sight until they are summoned.

For this activity, have kids get on their hands and knees and pretend to be sheep. Older children might prefer to be an audience as the younger children portray the sheep. Tell the kids you'll be describing some ways sheep behave and that you want them to act out what you say. Have kids say "baa" whenever you pause in the story.

Say: **David was responsible, and this pleased God. Let's look more closely at what David did to become known as responsible and trustworthy.** Hold up your Bible. **Young David's story is found in 1 Samuel 16 and 17. Sheep, remember to act out what I tell you about sheep, and watch how your shepherd David takes care of you.** Read the "Shepherd Duties" story (p. 35) as the children act our their roles.

Congratulate the kids for a great acting job. Gather all your children inside the sheep pen you created during the story. Say: **David was faithful to his shepherd responsibilities and to practicing his harp. He earned the trust of**

God and others. And David was given more important jobs to do. In fact, God had already chosen David for something very important. Eventually, David became the king of all Israel—the greatest king Israel ever had. Ask:

● **How do you think these shepherding responsibilities helped David become a good king?**

● **How have your earlier responsibilities prepared you for jobs you have now?**

● **How might the responsibilities you have now help you get ready for other things God has planned for your future?**

● **What other bigger responsibilities would you like to be trusted to do now or when you're older?**

Say: **It's a good feeling to be trusted by others, but it's not always easy to be faithful to our responsibilities. It wasn't easy for David either. The Bible tells us of many times David called on God for help. We can ask God to help us with our everyday responsibilities. We can be responsible with God's help.**

Turn to a partner, and tell that person one thing it's hard for you to be responsible about. Allow about one minute for sharing.

Say: **Now close your eyes and think about one good thing that might come from doing that particular job well.** Allow kids about thirty seconds of quiet time to think, then about thirty seconds to share their thoughts with the same partners if they would like to.

(10 minutes)

racing AHEAD

Each child needs one or two washed, flat stones about the size of golf balls. You'll also need crayons and some type of heating source: an oven, a toaster oven, or an electric skillet.

Say: **We're going to make Rock Reminders. First you'll need to color designs on your rocks using at least two colors on each rock. Then we're going to heat your rocks and find out what happens to your designs. It's a surprise!**

Preheat an oven to 450 degrees (or set a toaster oven or electric skillet to the highest temperature). Place the crayon-covered rocks on a cookie sheet, and heat them for three to five minutes. While the rocks are heating, say: **These rocks are feeling lots of heat, just as you "feel the heat" when the pressures of your responsibilities build up inside of you. What do you think will happen to these rocks?**

Remove the tray of rocks, and let the kids look, but not touch because the rocks will still be hot. The wax will have melted and created an interesting effect. Ask:

● **How is what happened to our rocks like the change that takes place** in our lives when we stick to our responsibilities?

Say: **Use these rocks to help you remember how beautifully things can turn out for you when you continue being faithful to your duties. Kids can be responsible with God's help. And God honors kids' faithfulness.**

following the footsteps

(10 minutes)

After the rocks have cooled, let the kids gather them and sit in a circle.

Say: **In Matthew, chapter 25, Jesus tells a story about a master who gave three of his servants different jobs to do while he was away on a trip. The first two servants were so faithful to their duties that the master rewarded them and gave the servants even more important jobs to do after his return. But the third servant was irresponsible and didn't do the job his master had given him to do. The master took away all of this servant's responsibilities and gave them to the first servant, who had been the most responsible.** Ask:

● **How do you think the first two servants felt after the master trusted them with more important jobs to do?**

● **How do you feel when you're trusted to do important jobs?**

Say: **It feels good to be trusted, but it's difficult to always be responsible. So we're going to ask for God's help. Please pass your rocks to the person sitting to your right.** Pause. **Now silently ask God to help the person whose rocks you're holding to be faithful to his or her responsibilities.** Pause.

Close by praying this prayer together: **Dear Father, we thank you for trusting us with different responsibilities. It's hard sometimes to be faithful to what you've given us to do. We need your help, God. Please give us strength when we don't feel like finishing our homework, feeding our pets, or cleaning our rooms. Thank you, Father, for your help and love. Amen.**

 # Shepherd Duties

Shepherd David was out in the field, caring for his sheep. Every morning, his sheep waited for him. Pause. The sheep knew the sound of his voice. This particular morning, David was getting ready to lead his sheep further up the mountain to greener grass because the hot sun of summer had turned the grass brown. David, lead your sheep. Don't forget to call their names so that no one strays. You're traveling far from home. Sheep, you always follow your shepherd. Pause.

Suddenly, a lion appeared! The lion should pop out and roar. David should pretend to fight it off and kill it with his or her staff. Then David and his sheep were able to travel on in safety. On and on they traveled, and still they had not found green pastures.

Next came a bear. David knew what to do. Pause as David pretends to fight and kill the bear. That was good work, David. You just saved your sheep's life.

Sheep panic when they hear a sudden noise. If you have an audience, cue the audience to make a sudden noise. If not, bang a table and say: Go ahead, sheep, panic! Pause. But David stepped into the middle of the flock, and the sheep instantly calmed down. Pause. If David had not been there to calm the sheep's fears, the sheep could have run off into danger, maybe even right over a cliff.

The Bible tells us David was also a skilled harp player. So that means he must have spent hours practicing.

When do you think David had time to practice his harp? Pause for children's responses.

Finally, David found green fields. Sheep, go ahead and eat the green grass; David, you now have time to practice your harp. Pause.

Some days, playing his harp may have been restful and enjoyable to him. Other days, it may have felt like just another responsibility.

What jobs do you have that are enjoyable but sometimes seem like a big responsibility? Allow children time to respond.

Let me tell you about one more shepherding responsibility. When he was miles from home, David had to sleep outside with his sheep. At night he gathered his sheep into a fold-out pen without a door. Quickly make a pen using chairs. Call your sheep, and lead them into their pen, David. Pause. Then David lay in front of the opening. He slept there all night to protect the sheep from wild animal attacks. Pause.

This is a great time to sing any psalm song your children know, such as "The Lord Is My Shepherd."

The Little Slave Girl and Her Master's Big Problem

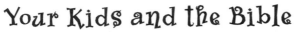

Kids Can know that God uses little things to bring about big changes.

Your Kids and the Bible

Small things mean a lot to kids. A pat on the back, a smile, or an encouraging word can brighten up a child's world. Conversely, a brief negative comment, a sneer, or simply not listening to a child can crush his or her self-esteem and cause a negative effect that lasts for days, months, or even years. God is well aware of the power of small gestures and of the magnitude of the changes they can bring about.

God used something as small as a slave girl's comment to significantly affect a mighty captain of the Aramaean (Syrian) king's army. The circumstances of her life did not set her apart as special. After all, she was just a slave, probably taken during one of the many border raids that Aram undertook against its enemy, Israel. She was forced into service to Naaman's wife. We do not know much about her, not even her name. She was probably seven to twelve years old—old enough to be useful for work and young enough to not be married. As a slave, her choices in life would have been few.

What we do know is that she chose to hold on to her faith in the God of Israel. The servant girl knew that God had placed her in Naaman's house for a purpose, and she remained faithful to God. Rather than see Naaman suffer the pain and shame of the disease of leprosy, she pointed out the only way he could be healed. She told her mistress about God's prophet, Elisha. It was the servant girl's little act of faith that brought about the big change in Naaman's life, his healing and his decision to follow the one and only true God.

During this lesson, your students will learn how God used a little girl with fewer choices than they have, and they will have an opportunity to think about how God can use them and their small acts to bring about big changes, too.

Simple Supplies

- clear vinegar, clear dishwashing liquid, food coloring, baking soda, clear plastic cups, foam plates, plastic spoons, and paper towels
- pita pocket bread (one for every two students)
- raisins
- white cheese sticks
- cornstarch baby powder or flour, a damp washcloth, and a sheet
- two plastic play hoops

- small paper sacks, stickers or stamps and ink pads, ribbon
- "necessaries" from the "Blessing Bag Items" (p. 43)
- scissors
- photocopies of "Blessing Bag Items" handouts (p. 43)
- newsprint (a six- to eight-foot-long piece)
- markers

focus FUN

(10 minutes)

Plan for one plastic cup, one foam plate, one cup of clear vinegar, and one plastic spoon for every four children. Before class, pour one cup of vinegar into each plastic cup, and add a squirt of dishwashing liquid. Stir the mixture gently so that the dishwashing liquid is undetectable. Place all the supplies in one area where the children can pick them up.

As kids arrive, have them form groups of four. Have the groups decide which person in each group will serve as the Construction Manager, the Mixer, the Secret Agent, and the Maintenance Engineer.

Give each Construction Manager a plate and a cup filled with vinegar. Have them place the cups exactly in the center of the foam plates on their work surface. Place three drops of food coloring in each cup, and ask the Mixers to stir gently. Give each Secret Agent about one teaspoon of baking powder on a paper towel, and give each Maintenance Engineer a supply of paper towels. Then have all the Secret Agents begin adding one pinch of the powder at a time to the liquid. After the kids have observed the reaction, have the Maintenance Engineers wipe up any spills and carry a trash can to their work spaces to dispose of the supplies. Ask:

teacher TIP:

The interaction of the vinegar and baking soda will cause a bubbly overflow. The dishwashing liquid intensifies the effect. Make sure that each group works in an uncarpeted area in case their plates overflow.

● How much powder did it take to start the reaction?

● What happened when you added more powder?

● If you've seen this experiment before, how was it different from other times you've seen it?

Say: **This experiment causes a chemical reaction. This time we supercharged the reaction by adding liquid detergent. Our Bible story today is about a servant girl who brought a tiny message, like the tiny amount of powder the Secret Agents dropped into the cups. Through her small contribution, God brought about an amazing reaction that changed the lives of many people. Today we are going to learn that God uses little things to bring about big changes.**

A Leap into the Bible

(20 minutes)

You will need baby powder, a damp washcloth, and a sheet (preferably blue).

Say: **Our Bible story today is found in the second book of Kings, chapter five. It's about a slave girl and her master, Naaman, who had leprosy. I'll need everyone's help in telling this story.** Choose someone to play the part of Naaman (NAY-uh-mun). Say: **Naaman was an important man in his country of Aram (AIR-um). He was a commander in the king's army. But he had a disease called leprosy. That disease would eventually cause him to be separated from his job, family, and friends. Leprosy is a disease that affects the skin. At first, it turns a person's skin white** (apply baby powder to Naaman's arms and face), **and in Bible times people were taught that it made a person "unclean." Unclean people had to live outside the gates of the city, away from everyone, until they were cured** (Leviticus 13:46).

I need someone to play the part of the slave girl and Naaman's wife. Show the servant girl the motions of sweeping with a broom and dusting, and have Naaman's wife pretend to rock a baby. Choose the rest of your actors, and show them their motions: the king of Aram and the king of Israel form "crowns" with their hands and place them on their heads, Elisha walks as though leaning on a stick, the messenger acts as if he or she is unrolling a scroll and reading from it, and Naaman's servants choose household chores to pantomime. Choose six children to hold the sheet, which will represent the Jordan River. (If your class is small, your actors can double up on parts.) The rest of the children can play the part of the band that captures the slave girl.

Now I am going to read the Bible story. Listen carefully for your part. When you hear me say that Naaman was strong and brave, Naaman will step up, flex his muscles, and act brave. Have Naaman practice. You may have to coach kids through the story, pointing to each actor at the appropriate time.

A long time ago in the land of Aram, there lived a man named Naaman. Have Naaman step forward. **Naaman was the commander of the army of the king of Aram. He was a great man in the king's eyes and was well liked.** Have Naaman proudly strut around. **The reason he was so well liked was because the Lord had given victory in battle to Aram through Naaman. Naaman was a brave soldier, but he had leprosy.** Have Naaman act sad.

Now bands from Aram had gone out (signal your band) **and kidnapped a young girl from Israel** (have them "kidnap" the servant girl), **and she was given to Naaman's wife as a slave.** Have the servant girl sweep while Naaman's wife rocks the baby. **One day the servant girl stopped and said to Naaman's wife** (have the girl stop sweeping and act as if she is talking to Naaman's wife), **"If only my master, Naaman, would see the prophet who is in Samaria! He would cure him of his leprosy."**

Naaman's wife must have told her husband about the servant girl's comment, because Naaman went to the king of Aram and told him what the slave girl from Israel had said. Have Naaman go to the king of Aram, and have them act as if they are talking.

The king of Aram said, "By all means, go. I will send a letter to the king of Israel. Have the king pretend to hand over an envelope. **So Naaman left to see the king of Israel.** Have Naaman walk around the room until he stands before the king of Israel and hands him the envelope. Have the king of Israel pretend to read the letter and then act very sad. **The letter that Naaman took to the king of Israel read, "With this letter I am sending my servant Naaman to you so that you can cure him of his leprosy." As soon as the king of Israel read the letter, he tore his robes.** Have the king pretend to tear his clothes and talk, acting very upset. **And he said, "Am I God? Can I kill and bring back to life? Why does this fellow send someone to me to be cured of his leprosy? See, he is trying to pick a fight with me by asking me to do something for him that I can't, even if I wanted to!"**

Have Elisha step forward. **When Elisha, the man of God, heard that the king of Israel had torn his robes, he sent a message to the king: "Why have you torn your robes? Have the man come to me and he will know that there is a prophet in Israel."**

So Naaman went to Elisha's door with all his horses and chariots. Have Naaman stand in front of Elisha and his messengers. **Elisha sent a message.** Have the messenger "read" the message. **The message said, "Go wash yourself seven times in the Jordan, and your flesh will be restored and you will be cleansed."** Have the children representing the river stretch the sheet between them. Have Naaman act as if the idea of washing in the Jordan is crazy.

Naaman went away angry and said, "I thought he would come out and stand over me and call on the name of His Lord—wave his hands over me and I would be cured! I have rivers at home in Damascus that are better than any here in Israel. Couldn't I wash in them and be cleansed?" So he

turned and walked away in a rage. Have Naaman stomp off, but have his servants stop him and act as if they are begging him.

Naaman's servants went to him and said, "My father, if the prophet had told you to do some great thing you would have done it. So you should do what he says when he tells you to do something as simple as wash and be cleansed." Naaman listened to them and went down to the Jordan River and dipped himself seven times as the man of God had told him, and his flesh became clean like that of a young boy. Have Naaman stand behind the sheet with you as the river rises and falls seven times. As the river moves, use the washcloth to clean all the powder off him. **Then Naaman and all his attendants went back to the man of God.** Have Naaman and his servants stand before Elisha. **Naaman said, "Now I know that there is no God in all the world except in Israel."** Have Naaman act as if he is happy.

Thank your actors, and applaud as they take their seats. Ask:

● **What was the small thing that started this whole series of events?**

● **How do you think the servant girl knew that God would use Elisha to cure Naaman?**

● **Why do you think she chose to tell her mistress about Elisha instead of keeping quiet and letting Naaman suffer?**

● **When we see someone suffering, what are some things we can say to them?**

● **What are some ways that God can use us to help others who might be hurting?**

Say: **Some of the things you mentioned were small things, things that might not seem very significant at the time. But God can use those kinds of little things to bring about big changes.**

A Walk in the Servant Girl's Shoes

(10 to 15 minutes)

Pull the pita bread apart so that you have two circular "plates" from each pocket. Have the children form pairs to be servant partners. Have one partner get the plate and the other put raisins and cheese on it.

When the kids are settled and eating their snacks, explain: **This was the kind of food that the servant girl probably would have eaten. She might also have eaten watermelon, fresh grapes, cucumbers, roast chicken, apples, nuts, pomegranates, figs, and eggs. She might have eaten fish if she lived close to a lake or a river or the coast. The pita bread was used as a plate and then eaten when the meal was finished. They did not use silverware as we do today. They used their fingers. They often dipped their bread into the dishes, picking up the food with the bread.**

Discuss with kids what the servant girl's life might have been like. Ask:

● **What chores do you think she might have had to do in Naaman's house?**

● **Where do you think she might have slept?**

● **How do you think she felt about not being able to choose an occupation when she grew up?**

After the children have finished eating, say: **We do not know for sure if she would have had time for many games, but she probably played one or two during her lifetime. We are going to play one based on a game that children might have played during her time period. Children in Bible times used hoops for various games. They were kind of like our play hoops. They were probably made from wood. We are going to play a relay game with our hoops.**

Have the children form two teams on one side of the room. Place two chairs at the opposite side of the room. Have the teams each form a straight line. Hand a play hoop to the first person in each line, and instruct them to roll their hoops on the floor toward and around their chairs, then back to the next person in line, and then be seated. Then the next person will roll the hoop around the chair and back. Continue until everyone has had a turn and is sitting on the floor.

teacher TIP:

If your weather permits, this is a great game to play outside where the children can safely run.

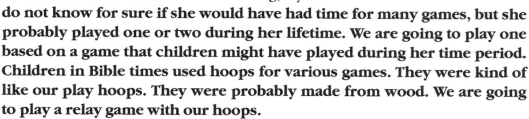

(10 to 15 minutes)

racing AHEAD

You will need small paper sacks; the necessaries you have chosen (see lists on page 43); ribbon; "Blessing Bag Items" handouts (p. 43), one for each Blessing Bag; scissors; writing tools; and stickers, ink stamps, or other items to decorate the bags.

Say: **The servant girl had an open faith. She was willing to share her faith as she worked. God used her brief comments to start a big change in Naaman's life.**

Because of our faith in God, we're going to do a little thing for some people and trust God to use it to make a big difference in their lives.

As a service project, your class will make up a bag full of necessaries for a shelter program in your area. Plan ahead to find out the shelter's greatest needs. If you have no local shelters, ask your pastor about the needs of missionaries in your denomination. Other options include creating surprise bags for the children's ward of a local hospital or bags for parents to have in their cars to give to those who carry "will work for food" signs. This service project could be easily adapted for a variety of situations by altering the contents of the sacks.

This project can be as elaborate or as simple as you want. You might be able to involve the whole congregation by printing in the bulletin a list of possible donations. You may choose just one or many items per bag. In either case, it is the experience that counts, not the number of items used.

Set up an assembly line with several stations.

Station 1: decorating the sacks. Set up the materials to decorate the sacks with pictures, ink stamps, or stickers.

Station 2: stuffing the bags. Lay out the items you will put in the bags so that children can easily place one of each inside.

Station 3: tag-it and tie-it. Have an older student with neat handwriting fill in the name of your church on the Blessing Tag and attach it to the bag. Tie the bag with a ribbon.

Collect all the bags for distribution.

Discuss with the students the difference a few necessaries can make in a person's life when the person doesn't have them. Have kids imagine having no home in which to sleep, bathe, or even brush their teeth. Say: **These blessing bags that you are providing might make the difference that helps someone get a job or just feel better after washing up. These blessing bags might lead someone to allow God into their lives. We will have faith in God that he will use our little gestures to make a big change in someone's life!**

following the footsteps

(5 minutes)

Say: **Today we have been learning about small things that God can use to make big changes. We saw how adding a little baking soda to vinegar makes a big, bubbly change. We heard about a little servant girl who said one small thing and enabled a brave army commander to be cured and begin to serve God. We also added several small things to our Blessing Bags with faith that God will use them to make a big change in someone's life.**

Lay a sheet of newsprint on the floor along with the markers.

Say: **I have a blank piece of paper on the floor that we will hang on the wall later. This is your chance to write, draw, and color your ideas of some small things you can do to allow God to make a big change in your life or the lives of those around you. For example, if you know there is a new kid moving into a home near yours, you might take the time to stop by to say hello. What might happen as a result?**

When God is part of the little things we do, he can use those simple words or actions to bring about enormous changes! When the students have finished, hang the mural on the wall and discuss the different ideas that the children have conveyed there.

Close with a circle of prayer thanking God for small things that make a big difference and asking for help in seeing more opportunities to do the small things.

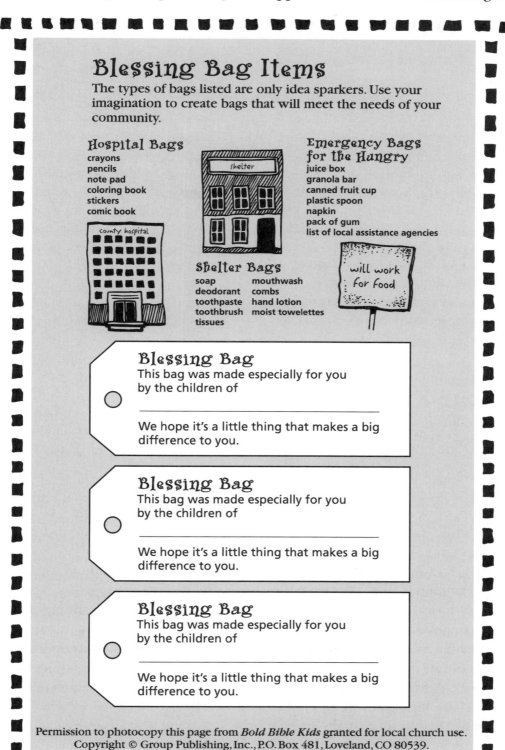

Blessing Bag Items

The types of bags listed are only idea sparkers. Use your imagination to create bags that will meet the needs of your community.

Hospital Bags
crayons
pencils
note pad
coloring book
stickers
comic book

County hospital

shelter

Emergency Bags for the Hungry
juice box
granola bar
canned fruit cup
plastic spoon
napkin
pack of gum
list of local assistance agencies

will work for food

Shelter Bags
soap   mouthwash
deodorant   combs
toothpaste   hand lotion
toothbrush   moist towelettes
tissues

Blessing Bag
This bag was made especially for you
by the children of
_____
We hope it's a little thing that makes a big
difference to you.

Blessing Bag
This bag was made especially for you
by the children of
_____
We hope it's a little thing that makes a big
difference to you.

Blessing Bag
This bag was made especially for you
by the children of
_____
We hope it's a little thing that makes a big
difference to you.

Do the Right Thing! Josiah, the Boy King

Kids Can choose to live according to God's Word no matter what kind of examples they have.

Your Kids and the Bible

Josiah became a king at the ripe young age of eight after his father, Amon, was assassinated by his own officials (2 Kings 21:23). The story of life in Judah (the southern kingdom of Israel) at this time reads like a modern soap opera. The people in Judah were led astray by many evil kings before Josiah. Altars and poles of worship for false gods were spread throughout the land. Cult prostitution, child sacrifice, and other pagan practices had been adopted by the Israelites.

Josiah rejected the examples of his father and grandfather and chose instead to follow God with his whole heart and soul. At the age of sixteen, he began to seek God. By the time he was twenty, he ordered the destruction of all the pagan poles and altars in the land (2 Chronicles 34:3-7).

Josiah's decision to follow God was probably influenced by his mother as well as the officials in the palace who helped raise him. This story offers tremendous hope for children today who may or may not have good role models to follow at home. These children can be encouraged to follow God by you, their Sunday school teacher; by a Christian day-care provider; or even by a caring neighbor or baby sitter who will take the time to share with them.

Simple Supplies

- Bible
- crayons
- scissors
- tape or glue
- dark bedsheets or blankets
- simple musical instruments such as cymbals, sticks, recorders, or kazoos (If you don't have these, kids can slap their thighs, whistle, or snap their fingers!)

- grapes and pomegranates (grapes only if pomegranates are not readily available)
- child-sized robes or other simple king and queen mother costumes
- photocopies of the "Josiah's Crown Choice" handout (p. 52)
- photocopies of the "Choices to Make" handout (p. 51) (cut apart)

(5 minutes)

focus FUN

Say: **Today we are going to learn about Josiah, the boy king who followed God even though his father had set a bad example. Josiah's father's name was King Amon. While we play the game, try to follow the directions even when I don't give you a good example. I'll pretend to be King Amon, and all of you will pretend to be Josiah. The game is a lot like Simon Says, so when I tell you an action like, "King Amon says, 'Touch your toes,' " follow along. Remember, if I only say, "Touch your toes" without saying, "King Amon says," then you should not do what I say. Ready?**

King Amon says, "Touch your toes."

Read your Bible.

King Amon says, "Blink your eyes."

King Amon says, "Touch your head."

Bow down and worship God.

King Amon says, "Hop on one foot."

King Amon says, "Stop hopping."

King Amon says, "Turn in circles."

Stop turning and look to God.

King Amon says, "Stop turning and look up."

Raise your hands up to God.

King Amon says, "March in place."

Wonderful job! Ask:

● **What did you notice about all of the commands I gave that didn't mention King Amon?**

● **Why do you think that the King Amon commands never mentioned God?**

● **How is that like some people's lives today?**

King Amon was Josiah's example, just as adults today are examples for children. Some people are great examples and point us to God's loving ways. Others, like King Amon, set an example that is not good or right in God's eyes. Josiah's life shows us that kids can live according to God's Word no matter what their examples are like.

(10 to 15 minutes)

A Leap into the Bible

Gather children at a table. Distribute one "Josiah's Crown Choice" handout (p. 52) to each child in your class, and make sure each one has crayons and scissors.

Say: **We're going to make a tool to help us with today's Bible story. Color the crown, and then make it the right size for your head.** As the students decorate and cut out their crowns, explain to them that Josiah was an eight-year-old king of Israel who made a great choice to follow God. When the children have finished their crowns, have children put them on with the dark side facing forward. When an older child has finished, have him or her open a Bible and read aloud 2 Chronicles 34:1-3, 29-33 to the rest of the

class. After everyone has heard a few verses about Josiah, show the students how to use their crowns to help act out the whole story of Josiah's life. Have children watch for you to signal by raising your hand, and then spin their crowns so that the color on the front of their crowns agrees with the story as you read it.

After you have finished the story "Do the Right Thing" (p. 47), ask:

● **How do you think God felt about the kings who led his people in evil ways?**

● **Why do you think the kings before Josiah chose to live in evil ways?**

● **Who do you think helped Josiah choose to follow God or do the right thing?** The answer to this is probably the palace officials who helped to raise Josiah both before and after his father's death. The Bible doesn't tell us this important detail, but let your kids offer suggestions about who influenced Josiah, such as his teachers, his friends, or maybe his mother or younger brothers or sisters.

teacher TIP:

You might want to have the older students in your class help the younger students cut out and tape or glue their crowns.

● **Why is it sometimes hard for us to do the right thing and follow God today?**

● **How can we choose to follow God despite the bad examples in our lives?**

Say: **Josiah had some really poor examples of how to be a king. Today some kids don't have very good examples of right living either. But Josiah's life shows us that kids can choose to live according to God's Word no matter what their examples are like.**

Let's play a game to learn more about carefully choosing our leaders.

This fun variation of the simple game Follow the Leader called Follow the King will illustrate an important truth about carefully choosing leaders. You will need to set up a "dark room" before class. Drape blankets over a table in your classroom, or use an already darkened area near your classroom. Make sure that your dark room is large enough to accommodate approximately half the students in your class.

Choose a student in your class to help lead this game. The student volunteer will play King Josiah, and you will play King Amon. Have the students choose which king they would like to follow. Try to encourage balanced teams, but don't worry too much about exact numbers. Lead the children in a wandering walk around the room, and have them repeat the following chants. The followers of King Josiah should chant, "Yahweh, Yahweh, I will follow God's way!" The followers of King Amon should chant, "My way, my way, I will go my own way!"

After children have wandered around the room in your two lines for a while, lead the followers of Amon to the dark room. Squeeze everyone together, and shut the door or close the blanket flap. Encourage King Josiah to lead his followers over to your group and chant, "Darkness, darkness, we choose light!" At this point, open the door or remove the blankets, and let the followers of Amon leave the dark room.

Do the Right Thing!

Long, long ago in the southern part of Israel, kings ruled over the people. Sometimes these kings loved God and led the people in God's ways. Signal kids to turn their crowns so that the gold crowns face forward. **At other times, evil kings led the Israelites in evil ways.** Signal kids to turn their crowns so that the dark crowns face forward. **They learned these evil ways from the people who lived around them. Sometimes the kings would marry women from the tribes around Israel and follow the false gods that these tribes worshipped. They passed these evil ways on from father to son. The evil kings had names like Manasseh (mah-NASS-uh) and Amon. Amon was so evil that the people who worked for him decided to kill him.**

When Amon died, his young son, Josiah, who was only eight years old, became the king. Because his father died, Josiah was raised primarily by palace officials such as the Royal Steward and the Royal Secretary. While he was growing up, Josiah had a choice to make: Would he follow God (gold crown), or would he follow the evil ways of his father and grandfather (dark crown)? Josiah made a wise choice to do the right thing and follow God with his whole heart and soul (gold crown). The Bible tells us that he made that choice when he was sixteen years old. It also tells us that when he was twenty years old, he ordered the people to tear down the idols and altars that his father and grandfather had set up to worship false gods.

Later, Josiah was supervising some work on God's Temple when his workers found the book of the Law that Moses had written. It was a treasure that had been hidden for many years. Josiah was so pleased to find it that he gathered all the people together and read it aloud to them. When the Israelites heard Josiah read God's Word to them, they pledged to follow it, and return to the ways of the one true God.

A Walk in Josiah's Shoes
(10 minutes)

Say: **In order to better understand what it would have been like to live in the palace with Josiah, let's role play a palace scene.** Set up the biggest chair in the room as the throne, and have a volunteer step up to the throne to play the part of King Josiah. Next choose a volunteer to play the part of the queen mother, Jedidah (jih-DIGH-duh). Then select several children to be palace musicians, and give them simple instruments to play. Next choose a Royal Steward to take charge of the whole palace. Then find a Royal Secretary to be responsible to clean up and organize all the books in your classroom. Appoint a cupbearer to taste all of the king's food before he eats it to make sure that it is not poisoned. The rest of the children in your class may play the parts of the king's bodyguards. The primary activity to role play will be snack time in the royal palace. Have the Royal Steward clap his or her hands and announce snack time for everyone. Have the cupbearer bring a plate of grapes and pomegranates to the king and carefully sample the food before the king eats any. After the king has been served, have the bodyguards help serve the fruit to all of the other members of the royal court. Ask:

● What would you have liked about living in the palace with King Josiah?

● What would you miss about living in our country today?

● Think about all the people Josiah saw daily at the palace. How do you think Josiah felt about them?

● How do you think he felt about his father's example?

● What do you think influenced Josiah's choices the most?

● How have you seen those same things influence some of your friends?

Say: When kids don't have good examples from the adults they are closest to, they sometimes look toward adults who are following God's plans, such as teachers, pastors, or baby sitters. Sometimes, kids learn about God from the Bible and decide they are going to live according to God's Word no matter what anyone else is doing. We don't know which of those is true for Josiah, but we know that he made right choices. His life shows us that we can live according to God's Word no matter what kinds of examples we have.

(5 to 10 minutes)

racing AHEAD

Say: We have a choice to make about how we will live our lives just as Josiah did in his day. We can follow the evil ways of the people around us at school or in our neighborhood, or we can choose to follow God. Think about someone who is setting an example you think would be right to follow.

● What are some things that person does that let you know he or she is living according to God's Word?

● Who or what can we *always* trust to help us make right choices?

When Josiah made a commitment to serve God, he established great worship for his people. Let's sing a song of commitment called "I Have Decided to Follow Jesus." After the class has finished singing the song, have everyone turn to a neighbor, shake his or her hand, and say, "Good choice!"

following the footsteps

(10 minutes)

Have your students form pairs and give each pair one real life choice from the "Choices to Make" handout (p. 51). Tell pairs that they will read about a life situation in which they have to make a choice. Have the children use the Rock, Scissors, Paper game to decide who will pantomime the right choice. (Rock takes scissors; scissors take paper; paper takes rock.) After one child has pantomimed the right choice, have the other person pantomime the wrong choice.

Ask:

teacher TIP:

Be sure that each pair has an older child who can read. If you don't have enough older children and readers in your class, form trios for this activity.

● If no one was watching your actions, what would you really have done in that situation? Why?

Our choices say a lot about how we feel about God. If we've decided to follow God, then our daily choices will usually honor him. Josiah decided to follow God, even though he was very young and even though he'd had really bad examples of how to live and rule his people. He said he would "follow the Lord and keep his commands, regulations and decrees with all his heart and all his soul" (2 Chronicles 34:31). He learned God's ways by reading God's words.

Have kids form multi-age groups of three to five. Say: **Earlier, we sang the song "I Have Decided to Follow Jesus." In your group, use the same tune to tell us what else you have decided to do, even if the examples you see are not so good.** Give the kids about three minutes to make up some new lyrics. Then have the groups sing their new songs to one another.

Say: **We can choose to live according to God's Word, no matter what our examples are like.** Pray together in closing.

Dear God, thank you for giving us wonderful examples in the Bible of kids who made good choices. Please help us to follow you with our whole hearts as Josiah did. Please bring people into our lives who are good examples, who will encourage us to read the Bible and follow your ways for the rest of our lives. In Jesus' name, amen.

Choices to Make

God is asking us to follow him today. Put yourself in the following situation, and pantomime what you would do.

Mom left a plate of cookies on the table to cool for a few minutes. She asked you not to eat any of them because you are going to take them to the new family who just moved in across the street. Mom leaves the kitchen to go change clothes. What will you do?

God is asking us to follow him today. Put yourself in the following situation, and pantomime what you would do.

You weren't ready for the spelling test your teacher said you were going to take this morning. Your neighbor is a spelling ace, and you can see his paper just fine from where you are sitting. What will you do?

God is asking us to follow him today. Put yourself in the following situation, and pantomime what you would do.

On your way to the playground, you see some older, tough kids beating up the small kid from down the street. If you don't join them and call him some names, you might be the next target. What will you do?

God is asking us to follow him today. Put yourself in the following situation, and pantomime what you would do.

Somehow you and a friend who were playing in the living room broke a vase. To avoid the consequences, you are tempted to blame the family cat. What will you do?

Josiah's Crown Choice

Color this side of the crown with dark colors such as brown, black, or purple.

I will follow other gods.

I Will Follow God.

Color this side of the crown gold.
Color the jewels beautiful, bright colors.

Jeremiah's Big Job in Judah

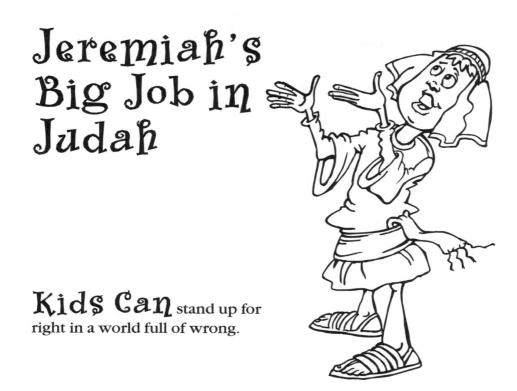

Kids Can stand up for right in a world full of wrong.

Your Kids and the Bible

Our world today is quite similar to the world Jeremiah lived in for most of his life. As adults in the Western world, most of us are accustomed to a life of religious freedom; in some cases, we have even witnessed revival at some point in our lifetime. Jeremiah grew up in a time of revival under the leadership of King Josiah. He was probably well grounded in his faith and used to sharing it openly with others. After Josiah died and his sons took over the throne, Jeremiah's religious freedoms were taken away, and he actually ended up being persecuted and thrown into prison for preaching the Word of God. Throughout the book of Jeremiah, he is the lone messenger proclaiming God's judgment in a world full of evil.

Jeremiah was probably in his late teens when God began giving him messages to speak to the people of Judah. However, his first response to the call of God was "I do not know how to speak; I am only a child" (Jeremiah 1:6). We need to help our children recognize that they are never too young to stand up for God.

It is also important to remember that children's early decisions help to prepare them for the time when God may have a special job for each of them to do. God had chosen Jeremiah for a big job in Judah, and God has chosen each of us to do a big job for him, too!

We need to show our kids practical ways that they can stand up for right in a world full of wrong. Our job as Christian teachers is to ground our kids in God's Word and give them practical ways that they can apply God's laws to their own lives. They need to be armed with the courage and commitment of Jeremiah. God will be with them even if they are "only children." He will help them be faithful in our world today.

Simple Supplies

- twelve containers of any kind (six per team)
- twelve pennies (six per team)
- two packs of M&M's for the kids to share (enough for the whole group)
- a treat (or drink) to share during the "Turn Back Now!" game
- a small lump of modeling clay for each child
- a pitcher of water (to test clay creations)
- a nontoxic marker
- a glass of water
- an eyedropper or straw
- a box of tissues

focus FUN

(10 minutes)

Before kids arrive, set up six of the containers on one side of the room and the other six on the opposite side. Allow enough room for one-half of the kids to sit in a circle around each set of containers. As kids arrive, direct them to one side of the room or the other. (You could divide the group into boys and girls or younger kids and older kids—the less equal the two groups, the better for this activity.) While children are waiting, ask them:

- **What do you think we will use these containers for?**
- **What would be your favorite thing to put in these containers?**

When most of the children have arrived and you are ready to begin, tell the kids that they will be playing the M&M Game. Tell them that you will give each group six pennies to toss into the containers. It does not matter how many pennies go into each container. Kids will need to stand up and take two steps back to play this game. When all six of the pennies are in the containers, the group should sit down and yell, "M&M's, please!" Tell them that you have a treat for the group that is first to get all the pennies in the containers.

Distribute the pennies and yell "Go!" When one of the groups has successfully tossed all its pennies into the containers and is sitting down yelling, "M&M's, please!" tell this group that you are going to give the other group a second chance to get their pennies into the containers. Be prepared for the first group to complain that this is not fair. Encourage the first group to cheer the other group on until all its pennies are in the containers. Pass out the M&M's for both groups to share.

Ask kids in the first group how they felt when you gave the second group another chance.

Ask kids in the second group how they felt when you gave them another chance.

Say: **In our Bible story today, the people of Judah had been doing bad things for a long time, and God wanted to give them another chance to turn back to him. Just as we gave the second group a chance to try again, God wanted to give the people of Judah a second chance, too. God used a young man named Jeremiah to give the people of Judah another chance to turn back to him before he punished them for their sins. Jeremiah was glad that God wanted them to have another chance, but none of the people wanted to give up sin and turn back to God. Even the leaders of the churches and the kings of the countries did not want to stop doing wrong. This made Jeremiah very sad and God very sad, too. The people did not want to take advantage of their second chance.**

A Walk in Jeremiah's Shoes
(15 minutes)

Say: **God chose Jeremiah to have the special job of being a prophet, a messenger for God. Jeremiah was also familiar with the job of a potter.** Hand out a small lump of clay to each child. **A potter took a lump of clay and formed different pots and containers out of it. The potter would put a lump of clay on a flat wheel and shape the pots and jars out of the clay as it was spinning on the wheel. The people could then use these pots and jars in their homes for drinking and storing things like oil and water.**

God told Jeremiah to go to the shop where the potter was making clay pots and jars. While Jeremiah was there, the potter had a problem with the jar he was making, and he had to squash the jar back into a lump of clay and start again. God

teacher TIP:

As an extra project for some of the older children, you can have them read Jeremiah 18:1-10 to find out how God used the illustration of the potter and the clay to give a message to the people of Judah. A second object lesson is described in Jeremiah 19:1-3, 10-11 where God tells Jeremiah to use a clay jar to show the people what will happen to them if they do not turn from their evil ways. After the older children have finished reading, they can report back to the group.

explained to Jeremiah that he, God, is like a potter who was making something out of his people in Judah. Ask the kids:

● **How is your life like this lump of clay?**

Say: **Let's see if you can make something out of your lump of clay that will hold water.** Give the kids a chance to work on this while you get the pitcher of water to pour into their "creations" to see if they will hold water. If they don't, instruct them to squash them down and try again, just as a potter would have to do if a clay pot was not turning out right.

Say: **God wanted the people to understand that he is like the potter and could reshape their lives into something good if they would turn away from their sinful ways. However, if they chose not to turn back to him, he would have to punish them and start again, just as the potter did. Jeremiah had to stand up for God and give people a message they didn't necessarily want to hear. Jeremiah's story helps us to know that we can stand up for right in a world full of wrong.**

Ask:

● **What are some messages from God's Word that might be difficult for people to hear?**

● **Suppose that God doesn't ask you to use words to take his message to people in the same way Jeremiah did. How else can you stand up for what's right?**

(10 minutes)

A Leap into the Bible

As you tell the story, you'll challenge kids with open-ended questions about how they would feel in situations similar to Jeremiah's. If you have a very young group, you can tell the kids to show you how they would feel by making faces (such as glad, sad, scared) as you ask the questions. Tell them they can use their faces and hands but no words are allowed. If your group is large, give children thirty seconds to share their feelings with partners.

Say: **Before we begin our story today, I want you to know that I am going to ask you some questions as I talk to you. After I ask each question, I am going to give you thirty seconds to show me how you feel** (or share how you feel with a partner, depending on which method you choose.) **Do any of you have a question about what to do?**

Begin the story: **God had a big job for Jeremiah to do. He wanted him to tell all the people in Judah that they should stop doing wrong things such as worshipping idols. God wanted Jeremiah to give the people another chance to turn back to their one true God who loved them and made them.**

Think about a time you were doing something wrong and someone asked you to stop doing wrong and do right instead. Think about how you felt when that happened. Pause to give kids time to think about their responses or to share.

teacher TIP:

In a smaller group setting (six to eight kids), allow time for a brief discussion after each question. Keep the discussion going so that your group doesn't lose track of the story's sequence.

Jeremiah was quite young when God gave him this big job to do. Jeremiah wasn't immediately enthusiastic about God's idea. He pointed out to God that he was "only a child" and God had asked him to go in front of important people like kings and rulers. God wanted him to tell the people in charge of the schools and the churches things that might really make those people angry. In fact, he'd even have to try to tell his family and friends to change their ways. Ask:

● **How would you feel if you had to tell someone important like a president or a prime minister that he or she should stop doing wrong things?** Pause for responses. You may have to remind younger kids that they are only to make a face to show how they would feel.

● **How would you feel if you had to tell your dad and mom that they were doing something wrong and that God wanted them to stop doing it?** Pause.

● **Now think about your best friend. How would you feel if you had to tell your best friend to stop doing something wrong?** Pause.

Say: **For some of us, it would be pretty hard to tell some of these people that they were doing something wrong. Jeremiah knew that it would be hard for him, so he told God that he was too young to do this big job.**

● **Tell about a time you felt you were too young to do something that your parent or teacher asked you to do.** Pause.

Say: **Even though Jeremiah had reasons for not wanting this task, God had chosen Jeremiah to carry his message. God wanted to give the people one last chance to be forgiven and turn back to him.**

● **Do you remember a time your mom or dad or a teacher said, "This is your last chance…"?** Pause for responses.

● **Why do you think God wanted to give his people another chance?**

Say: **Remember, Jeremiah thought he was too young to do the big job** that God wanted him to do. But God told him, "Do not say, 'I am only a child.' You must go to everyone I send you to and say whatever I command you. Do not be afraid of them, for I am with you and will rescue you" (Jeremiah 1:7-8). Because God was with him, Jeremiah had the courage to do God's work—to stand up for right. Jeremiah shows us that we can stand up for right in a world full of wrong.

 (20 minutes)

Say: **Let's play a game called Turn Back Now!** Have children form two equal lines. Have one line move close to the wall on one side of your room. Tell children that the people in the line closest to the wall will be the "Jeremiahs" (point to them) and the people in the line on the other side will be the "people of Judah" (point to them). If there is an uneven number of children, the extra child can team up with one other person in either line or lead the Jeremiahs in saying their line, "Turn back now!"

Instruct the two lines to face each other. Kids should be standing directly across from each other so that each person of Judah faces his or her own Jeremiah. Have the people of Judah turn and face away from the Jeremiahs and then take five giant steps away. With great fanfare, place the treat so that the people of Judah are facing it.

Say: **When I call out a challenge, the Jeremiahs** (point to them) **will try to influence the people of Judah with the words, "Turn Back Now!" The people of Judah will have to make a choice to take one step toward the treat or to turn around and take one step toward Jeremiah. Peo-**

ple of Judah, each of you must decide for yourself which you want to do. You can either obey the Jeremiahs or go your own way.

Begin reading from the list of challenges below. Let the kids decide to walk their own way (toward the treat) or Jeremiah's way (turning around and going toward their Jeremiahs). As each child reaches Jeremiah, hand him or her and the partner a treat from those that were placed across the room.

LIST OF CHALLENGES

● **You take a pencil from your friend's desk without telling him. You decide to keep it because it's such a good pencil and you need one.**

At first you may have to coach the Jeremiahs to yell, "Turn back now!"

● **Your mother tells you to turn off the light and get to sleep, but you decide to read your book a little longer.**

● **You know you should put the money that your mom gave you into the offering basket, but you would rather save it to buy a candy bar later.**

● **You see your friend sneak a small toy from the store when nobody is looking, but you decide not to say anything to her about it.**

● **Your friend wants you to give him the answers to some homework questions because he has hockey practice after school. You decide to help your friend even though your teacher said to do your own homework.**

● **Your coach couldn't see whether the ball was fair or foul, so to help your team out, you tell him it was fair even though you know it really wasn't.**

● **You get mad at your little sister and trip her but then lie to your mom and say it was just an accident.**

● **You tell the baby sitter that your mom said you could watch a certain television show, even though your mom has said it is off-limits.**

● **You pay your little brother twenty-five cents to keep his mouth shut and not tell your dad that you went to the store on your own after school.**

Ask the people of Judah:

● **Were you confused about which way to go? Why?**

● **When did it become clear to you that turning back to Jeremiah was the best way to go?**

Ask the Jeremiahs:

● **How did it make you feel when Judah was going away from you?**

● **How did you feel when your partner started coming back toward you.**

Ask the people of Judah:

● **Why did you decide to turn back to Jeremiah?**

Say: **Sometimes it looks as though walking our own way offers the greatest reward. The people Jeremiah was sent to certainly thought so! But in the end, just as in our game, the rewards come from paying attention to God's warnings. With God's help, we can stand up for right in a world full of wrong.**

(5 minutes)

Say: **Jeremiah is known as the "weeping," or crying, prophet. He was so sad about the sins of the people of Judah that he actually cried when he thought about the wrong things they were doing and how God was going to punish them. Let's think about some things in our world that we know are wrong.** Tell the children to close their eyes and when they each think of something that would make God sad, to hold out one fist with the palm pointed down. Show them how to do this before they close their eyes. Tell them that you will be drawing something on their hands with a marker after they hold them out. When they hold out their hands, draw on each hand two dots for eyes on the outside of the pointer finger on either side of the knuckle connecting the finger to the hand. (See illustration.)

After all children have eyes drawn on their hands, tell them to open their eyes, and show them how the dots make a little face on each of their hands. The two dots are eyes, and each student can move his or her thumb around to make the mouth.

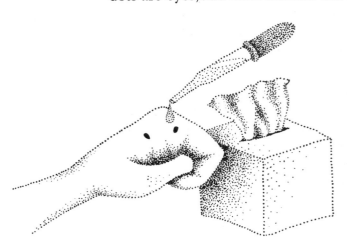

Say: **Now I'm going to put a little drop of water on the eyes of your little face to remind you that God is saddened by people turning away from him and his ways.** Use an eyedropper or straw to put a drop of water on the eyes of each child's hand. **Pass this tissue box around, and take a tissue to wipe away the tears. Tell a partner what you think would please God in the situation you thought about. For example, if you thought about crime you've seen in the news, you might tell your partner that God would be pleased if people turned back to him and there were more news stories about people doing good than bad. When your partner shares his or her thought, wipe the tears from the eyes on his or her hand.** Pass the tissue box around, and give kids several minutes to think about and share their ideas.

Say: **Those ideas you shared with your partner are right things that you can stand up for. Just as Jeremiah stood *against* the wrong things God showed him and stood up for what was right, you can stand up for right in a world full of wrong.**

End the lesson with this prayer: **Dear God, thank you for loving us and giving us chances to turn away from sin and back to you. Help us to remember that as your people, we can stand up for right in a world full of wrong. Amen.**

Daniel: A Boy With Integrity

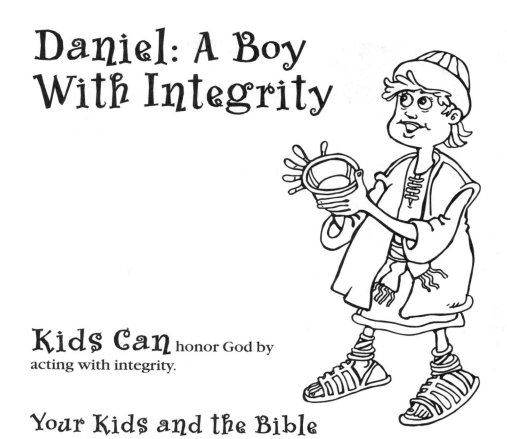

Kids Can honor God by acting with integrity.

Your Kids and the Bible

Daniel was a prophet, but not just one who could see the future in order to warn and encourage people to focus on God. Daniel was a prophet who knew how to live in such a way that showed others God was the one who *really* mattered. God's opinion made a daily difference in Daniel's life. Even though Daniel was taken from his family as a young man, he had already learned God's laws. He continued to communicate with God regularly, so he knew what God expected of him. Daniel gave his best in each situation because he knew that his personal efforts would draw attention to the God he served if he didn't compromise on the beliefs he learned at home.

Daniel's connection with God was like a red thread woven through a piece of gray fabric. It was easy to see. It was obvious against the backdrop of life as a captive in Nebuchadnezzar's court. Daniel's integrity called people around him to follow God's way instead of their own ways. Daniel sometimes found himself in some very difficult situations. One of them was when he asked the chief official for different food because he knew that the food of the court had been offered to idols. The food he was offered would have contaminated his soul, if not his body. God honored Daniel's courageous request with remarkable health.

Every day kids face choices about honoring God. Will they stand up for what's right or sit around and do nothing? Will they put God or their peers first? We learn from Daniel's example that right decisions can make a difference in the world we live in. In this lesson, kids learn that they can live as people of integrity, just as Daniel did.

Simple Supplies

- one plastic egg per child (You can substitute a resealable snack bag.)
- paper cut into 1x5-inch pieces
- Life Savers candies
- chalkboard and chalk, or newsprint and a marker
- craft foam (available in sheets from craft stores)
- wooden blocks (may be borrowed from the preschool class)
- plastic wrap
- scissors
- glue or glue sticks,
- "Cuneiform Letter Patterns" (p. 68)
- construction paper
- acrylic paint
- paintbrushes

(5 to 10 minutes)

 focus FUN

Before class, write the following phrases on strips of paper, wrap a Life Saver in each strip, and place each wrapped Life Saver in a plastic egg:

- at school
- at the mall
- at the theater
- at home
- at a friend's house
- at church

Make sure there is one egg per child (duplicate phrases are fine). Hide the filled eggs around the room your class meets in, or place them in a nearby room that has fun hiding places.

When the kids arrive, say: **We are going on a treasure hunt. There is a hidden treasure for each of you. When you find yours, don't open it. Just come back here and be seated. When everyone has come back, we'll explore our treasures together.**

When each child has found an egg and everyone is seated, have children open the eggs and unwrap the strips of paper inside. Encourage older kids to help younger children read the papers, and ask the children not to eat the candy yet. Ask:

- **What's valuable about what you found in your egg?**
- **What seems unimportant about what you found?**

Have several children read their strips aloud. Ask:

- **What similarities do you see in what is written on your papers?**

Say: **The similarity I want you to think about is that each is a place you might actually go and find an opportunity to honor God. You also found a small piece of candy—a Life Saver. We might be tempted to believe that the candy is more important than the piece of paper, just as we might be tempted to think that "saving our lives" (or people's opinions of us) is more important than the opportunity to honor God. Today we're going to learn about a man who believed that honoring God was more important than saving his own life and more important than what anyone else thought of him. His name was Daniel. Daniel honored God by doing his best. You can honor God by doing your best, too.**

Have kids put their eggs in a safe place, and ask them to think of ways they could honor God at the places listed on their papers. They will share their ideas later in the lesson.

A Walk in Daniel's Shoes
(15 to 20 minutes)

Say: **The story of Daniel began about six hundred years before Jesus was born. A Babylonian king named Nebuchadnezzar had conquered the people of Judah, who were Jews. He asked his most important court official to find some of the brightest young people from Judah and bring them back to his court so that they could learn all the customs of the Babylonians, including their language. Daniel was one of those chosen, and the Bible tells us he was a pretty terrific kid. As I describe what the Bible says about the kids who were chosen, I want you to position your body as though you are all those things. They were handsome (pause), quick to understand (pause), and well qualified to serve in the king's palace.**

As you stand there, imagine that you have all those great qualities. You have been taken from your loving family to learn the customs of another country so you can serve that country's king. Show me how you would feel by moving your body to reflect how you're feeling now. When kids have finished, have them be seated. Say: **I saw some of your whole bodies looking sad and depressed.** Ask:

● **What things would you try to remember about your home and family?**

● **Why do you think those things are important?**

Say: **Daniel remembered what his family had taught him, especially about God. As soon as he arrived at the palace, he began to show everyone there what was important to him. He stuck to what his family had taught him. Because Daniel stuck to what he had learned and believed, we say he had** *integrity*. **Throughout the rest of the lesson, when you hear me say the word "integrity," put your palms together in front of you** and act as if you are trying to pull them apart but they have glue on them. That's to help you remember that integrity is the character trait that helps us stick to what we believe. Let's practice. **Daniel had integrity.** (Pause for the action.) **Kids can have integrity.** (Pause for the action.) **Great! I think you really know that sticking with what you believe takes integrity.** (Pause.)

Daniel's integrity (pause) **helped him to honor God by doing his best at everything he was asked to do, including learning the language and customs of the Babylonians.** Write the word "integrity" on a chalkboard or a piece of newsprint.

Today we're going to learn a little about a language Daniel learned, Akkadian. The Akkadian language isn't used any more. It had its own written form, using a cuneiform writing system instead of the alphabet we're familiar with. We're going to create the letters that come the closest to our spelling of the word "integrity." Pause as the children do the motion for integrity.

Form seven groups, one for each letter. Give each group a three-inch square of craft foam, scissors, a wooden block, a piece of plastic wrap, glue or a glue stick, a paintbrush, a copy of one of the "Cuneiform Letter Patterns" (p. 68), and some acrylic paint. Show kids how to wrap the wooden block with plastic wrap to protect the surface of the block. Have kids work together in their groups to create cutouts of foam to glue onto the plastic-wrapped blocks. Each group will create a stamp that looks exactly like the copy of the letter pattern you have given them. When kids use the block to print with, they will create the Akkadian representation of each letter.

teacher TIP:

Instead of using construction paper, you could allow the kids to actually stamp these designs onto a slab of modeling clay, which is what the actual language that Daniel learned was written upon. If you choose this option, make sure the glue is dry before using the stamps.

When all kids have completed their block stamps, have each group place its pattern next to the stamp itself, so that other kids can identify which stamp represents each letter. Give each student a piece of construction paper, and have kids copy the word "integrity" from the sample on the chalkboard or newsprint. Show the kids how to use the paintbrush to apply paint to the stamps. Then tell them to go to each block and print the letters on their construction paper. Tell them that they don't have to print "I" first and "Y" last; they just need to get the letters in the right order as they rotate around the room.

Say: **Daniel's knowledge and understanding were amazing. He and his friends quickly learned to understand a language that was totally different from the one that they grew up speaking, writing, and studying as Jewish kids.** Ask:

● If you had to learn a new language, what do you think would be the hardest part for you?

● What other things would you need to know about the people you were living among (besides their language)?

Say: **The Bible tells us that Daniel learned even more about the people he lived among than they knew about themselves. Let's learn more about how God was honored by Daniel's efforts.**

(10 to 15 minutes)

A Leap into the Bible

Have the kids get their plastic eggs and sit down together. Say: **It was a unique time for a kid to grow up. Can you imagine being told to move to an entirely differ-** ent place and culture? **It wasn't just that Daniel and his friends were forced to move, but all of the things they did and ate were totally different in their new home. In fact, the king even tried to give Daniel a new name, after a false god who was worshipped in Babylon, so that Daniel would be less like a Jew. But in spite of all the challenges he faced, Daniel always remembered God's laws and chose to act with integrity.** Pause as the children do the motion for integrity.

Ask:

● **What are some of God's laws that you need to remember when you are away from your family or somewhere on your own?**

Say: **Long ago, God had given Daniel's ancestors rules about food. Food at Nebuchadnezzar's court was prepared and treated differently than the food in Daniel's family. The meat wasn't necessarily bad, but according to Jewish laws, it was unclean because it had been offered to false gods before it was delivered to Daniel to eat.** Have the kids take the candy from their eggs. Then have them stick out their tongues and place the candy on top, without eating it.

Say: **Eating unclean food in the king's court might have been as tempting to Daniel and his friends as it is to have a piece of candy on your tongue, knowing you've been told not to eat it. Now take the candy off your tongue, hold it with your fingers, and tell a partner how you feel about not being able to eat your Life Saver. Also tell your partner how your experience might be like or unlike Daniel's temptation to eat unclean food in Nebuchadnezzar's court.**

Allow about two minutes for sharing, and then say:

For Daniel to refuse to eat the food he was given meant that his life was actually in danger. He could have been killed for his disobedience. He chose to be true to the things he had learned at home and to eat only

those foods he knew were "clean"— fruits and vegetables. He acted with integrity (pause); he stuck to what he knew was right, even though it was hard. Daniel honored God. Do you know what God did for Daniel? God saved his life and gave him the ability to understand visions and dreams. This special gift would save his life more than once as he grew up and served the king of Babylon. To help you remember that God was Daniel's lifesaver, you may now, *finally*, eat the Life Saver treasure from your egg.

As kids eat, say: **You see, Daniel didn't worry about saving his own life. He did what was right, always did his best, and trusted God to be his lifesaver.**

● **Tell about a time you acted with integrity.**

● **How do you think God might be your lifesaver?**

Have the kids take the strips of paper from their eggs and get ready to share how they might honor God in the place listed on each strip.

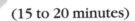

(15 to 20 minutes)

Have kids form opportunity groups of one or more students whose papers from the eggs say the same thing. For example, all the children who received a paper with the words "at school" will form one opportunity group.

Ask each group to create a TV commercial length skit (thirty to sixty seconds) that will show others where the opportunity is, what happens (the choice that is made), and how God is honored by the action. After each group performs its skit, ask the audience:

● **What was something the performers might have learned or decided ahead of time that helped them make the right choice in the skit?**

● **What might happen to others around them as a result of their actions?**

● **What if the performers had made the wrong choice?**

Say: **Just as Daniel honored God by doing his best and acting with integrity (pause), you can take advantage of the opportunities you have to honor God by doing your best. Sometimes it's tempting to be lazy, to take the easy way out, or to just not do what we know is right.** Ask:

● **How can we prepare ourselves to act with integrity (pause) when we have an opportunity?**

Say: **Daniel and his friends stuck together and helped one another be the best they could be to bring honor to God.**

● **What are some things you can do to help your friends do their best?**

following the footsteps

(5 to 10 minutes)

Form groups of four. Say: **Daniel was blessed to have that group of friends who were all brought into Babylon at the same time. Each of those friends had to make his own choices about honoring God, but it must have helped to know that he had others around him who believed the same things. Just as Daniel had his friends, we are blessed to have one another.**

Have each group of four stand back to back and link arms. Then have the groups be seated. Ask each student to say a prayer about integrity for the rest of the people in his or her group. Start with the person who is wearing the most blue, and move around the circle to the left. Tell the groups that when they have prayed for one another, they should all stand up together without letting go of one another's arms.

When all the groups are standing, say: **Each of you had to stand on your own, but you were helped by one another. Prayer is our way of helping strengthen one another's integrity so that God is honored. Think of one way you would like to honor God this week, and share it with your group.**

Close by leading the following group prayer. Pause after each line to allow kids to respond, "I'll give you my best!"

> **Dear Lord,**
> **In every opportunity** (I'll give you my best!)
> **I'll ask you what you want, and then** (I'll give you my best!)
> **I'll try to be like Daniel** (I'll give you my best!)
> **To honor you and please you, Lord,** (I'll give you my best!)
> **In Jesus' name, amen.**

Cuneiform Letter Patterns

Using these letter blocks, reproduce the word "INTEGRITY" with cuneiform blocks.

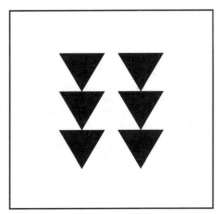

This will form "I."

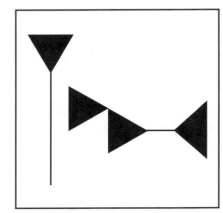

This will form "N."

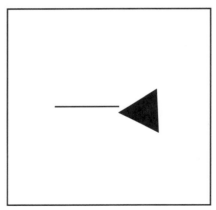

This will form "T."

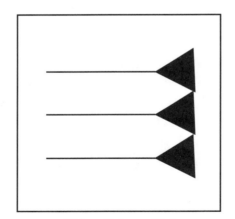

This will form "E."

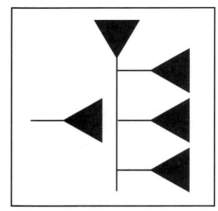

This will form "G."

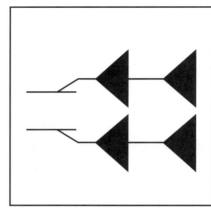

This will form "R."

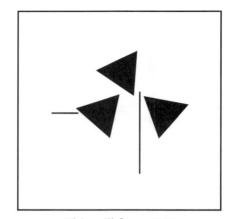

This will form "Y."

The Boy Who Shared

Kids Can share with others to show God's love.

Your Kids and the Bible

The crowd of people following Jesus had not given any advance thought to food. Perhaps they had intended to stay for only a short while and to be home in time for supper. But perhaps as they listened to the words of Jesus, they lost track of time and didn't even notice that mealtime was approaching.

The disciples worried about how to feed the crowd of more than five thousand, but Jesus had it all under control. He told the disciples to search the crowd for whatever food they could find. The disciples found only one person with food. A young boy had five small loaves of bread and two small fish. Although it was a seemingly insignificant amount of food for such a large crowd, the boy willingly shared what he had. Jesus used the little boy's offering and turned it into enough food for them all, plus enough for each disciple to collect a full basket of leftovers.

Jesus showed how he can use whatever we're willing to give. It was even more significant that he used the little a child brought. Kids often feel they have nothing to offer since they don't carry checkbooks and are usually dependent on others for what they do have. In this story, Jesus showed that if we are willing to share, he can use what any of us has to perform miracles.

Simple Supplies

- construction paper fish cut from several colors (one per child)
- paper and pencils
- brown lunch bags (one per child)
- newspapers or paper towels
- fish-shaped crackers
- a Bible costume (optional)
- a photocopy of the "Israeli Vegetable Stew" recipe card (p. 76)
- vegetable stew ingredients (one can black beans, one cup lentils, one cup instant rice, two tablespoons oil, one-fourth cup chopped onion, one teaspoon salt, and a dash of pepper)
- an electric skillet or Crock-Pot and a ladle
- a loaf of unsliced bread
- napkins, foam cups, and sandwich bags

teacher TIP:

To get their creative juices going, you may need to give your kids some ideas. For example, you might take three coins from your pocket and suggest something you can buy with them, then form them into a snowman, and then arrange them to represent eyes and a nose so kids can see a variety of possibilities. Your own creativity will set the tone for this activity.

focus FUN (10 minutes)

As children enter the classroom, give them each a construction paper fish. Then have them form teams based on the color of fish each person was given. After the teams have formed, ask the kids to search through their pockets and anything else they brought to class to find every tiny little thing they have with them. Have them place all these items on the floor in the center of their teams.

Say: **Look at all the things you have gathered. Use one or combine several things to come up with as many different possibilities for the items as you can. Don't be limited by the obvious! Be creative and brainstorm lots of ideas.**

Give kids about five minutes to work together. Then have each group share its top three ideas with the rest of the class. Say: **You had a chance to share what you have with the rest of your group. As you discovered, sometimes simple things can be used in interesting ways. Today** our Bible story is about a little boy who shared what he had. Jesus used the simple things he brought with him to make something *more* than interesting. He made something miraculous! As we learn about this boy, we'll learn that kids can share with others to show God's love.

A Walk in the Little Boy's Shoes

(10 minutes)

Say: **Today our Bible story focuses on the evening meal in the land of Israel. In that time, the evening meal was the biggest meal of the day. Breakfast was little more than a snack that the family ate on their way to work. Lunch was usually just bread and maybe fruit. The evening meal took place when the family was at home together. A typical dinner consisted of vegetable stew, bread, and milk. Meat was for the very rich or for special occasions.**

We're going to work together to prepare a simple vegetable stew like the stew the people in our story might have eaten if they'd been home. We'll let it cook while we do some other fun things.

Put the ingredients along with the recipe card on a table. Let children take turns adding each of the ingredients, and make sure everyone has a chance to stir the stew. Observe all safety precautions as you cook. Tape down the cord, and keep children a safe distance from the stew as it cooks. Cook it over low heat (or on high in a Crock-Pot). Stir it occasionally during the lesson. If you have a multi-age class, you can allow older children to take on this responsibility.

A Leap into the Bible

(20 minutes)

Before class, pad the brown lunch bags with newspaper or paper towels. In all the bags except one, include a slip of paper with the word "nothing" written on it. In the other bag, put an individual serving of fish-shaped crackers. Give each child a bag, and have kids put them aside until they are asked for them.

Say: **Today I've invited Andrew, one of Jesus' disciples to speak to us. Andrew was actually the one who found the young boy in the crowd and brought him to Jesus.**

Hello. I'm Andrew. You may know me as one of Jesus' disciples. At least I hope you do, because knowing Jesus was the best thing that ever happened to me. I spent three wonderful years serving Jesus and helping him as he needed me. One day, we decided that Jesus needed a break from all his teaching, so we headed out to a remote area of the countryside. We took a boat, but by the time we landed, people had already arrived and the quiet countryside didn't look so restful after all.

When Jesus saw all the people, he felt love in his heart for them, and he started teaching them. The crowd just kept growing until soon there were at least five thousand people there—and that was just the men! There were thousands more when you counted the women and children.

Soon it was mealtime. We disciples began to get a little concerned. You know what happens when that many people get hungry and tired and cranky. But we didn't have food for that many people. In fact, we didn't even have anything to eat ourselves. All of us disciples thought we should just send the people home so they could eat. But Jesus had another idea. He told us to go around and find out if anyone in the crowd had any food.

I really thought that was kind of a dumb idea, if you want to know the truth. It wasn't like anyone was going to just happen to have dinner for five thousand tucked under a napkin. Even if someone had enough for his or her family, it would only make the rest of the crowd more cranky. What good was it going to do to draw attention to one family who had plenty when the rest had nothing? But Jesus was smart enough to know the trouble that would cause, and he asked us to do it anyway. It was really kind of exciting, knowing Jesus had the situation under control. So, I started asking around.

A lot of people seemed surprised at the mention of food. They'd been so caught up in listening to Jesus teach that they hadn't even realized what time it was. Once they started thinking about food, they started to get a little restless, trying to figure out what they were going to do.

None of the adults had anything to eat, and we were getting discouraged. Then I noticed a crowd of kids in the back. I hesitated to go to them. I figured if none of the adults were prepared, surely those little kids had nothing. But I went to them anyway. When I asked them if any of them had any food, they started looking.

Look in your lunch sacks to see what they found. *(Pause for kids to look through their bags.)*

It happened a lot like that. Most found nothing. But one little boy found five small loaves of bread and two little fish. I took the boy straight to Jesus, but it still didn't make sense to me. I don't know what Jesus said to the boy, but he took the fish and bread and gave thanks to God for them. Then he told us to start serving.

So each of us took some and passed it out. Then we came back, and there was enough for another group and another and another, until the whole crowd had eaten. Not just a little bit— they ate until they were full! And there were leftovers! Even after it was all over, every disciple gathered up a big basket full.

You know, I'm not sure what would have happened if that boy had already eaten his food or if he hadn't brought anything at all. Jesus could have turned the rocks and grass into food if he'd wanted to. But it's just like Jesus to ask, "What do you have?" Because no matter how much or how little it seems we have, Jesus will take it and make it into much more than we could ever imagine. No matter what we have, we can share it with others to show God's love.

teacher TIP:

You can ask a volunteer to play the part of Andrew and read the monologue. Or, to add flavor to the drama, you can read the monologue yourself while dressed in a biblical costume. If you use one of the older children or a spur-of-the-moment recruit to perform the Andrew monologue, you can hide the script in a basket so that the actor can see it but the other children can't!

Say: **Thank you, Andrew, for sharing your story. Let's think about that story a little more.**

● **How do you think that little boy felt at the end of the day?**

● **What if that boy had thought, "If I give my food to Jesus, I'm sure going to be hungry. My mom packed it for me, and there's not enough for both of us!"**

● **What other thoughts do you think might have run through his mind?**

● **When have similar thoughts run through your mind?**

Say: **Bible scholars tell us that the kind of bread the boy had tells us that he was poor, so he probably didn't have much to share. But Jesus took what he did have and performed a miracle that still speaks to people today about his love and power. God uses a generous attitude. Like the boy in our story, you can share with others to show God's love.**

(10 minutes)

Have each child ladle soup into a foam cup and be seated on the floor. Explain to the children that families in Bible times didn't sit down at the table in most homes; they sat together on the floor. Break a piece of bread from the loaf for each child, and place it in a sandwich bag. Give the bags to the children, and ask them to hold them as you pray together.

After the prayer ask:

● **What's missing that you would ordinarily use to eat with?**

Say: **We have no spoons because the people of that day used bread as a spoon. But I have asked you not to eat your bread. How, besides lapping it from the cup, can you eat your stew?**

Let the kids struggle to come up with the idea of sharing their bread. Then say: **The only rule is that you must always leave enough bread in the bag to share with someone else.** Let the kids share their bread and eat their stew. If someone doesn't like the stew, encourage him or her to continue to share bread anyway. The experience can be a bit messy, so provide plenty of napkins.

After the kids have finished, say: **Look at your sandwich bag. What do you notice?** If the kids have followed the directions, they should still have some bread left in their bags.

Say: **Just as your bags aren't empty, God has a wonderful way of doing that very thing in our lives when we share with others. He makes sure that we never come up empty. Sometimes, he even does a modern-day miracle, and we end up with more than we started out with or maybe something completely different than we started out with—such as a wonderful feeling of happiness because we shared.** Ask:

● **When has something like that happened to you or someone you know?**

● **What plan could you have for sharing with others this week?**

Say: **God honors our generosity. We can share with others to show God's love.**

following the footsteps

(5 minutes)

Say: **Here's an opportunity for you to share in a simple way. Think of how old you are. That number is your special number today, and that is the number of things you get to give today. For example, if you are seven years old, you will try to give seven things to people in this class. Since you didn't come prepared with gifts, you will have to be creative with what you can give. For example, you can give smiles, hugs, compliments, or services. Try to give a different thing to each person, and try to share with as many people as you can. It's all right to go beyond your special number and share with even more people.**

Give the kids several minutes to accomplish this task. Remind them that their giving shouldn't end when they leave the room but that they can continue to share whatever they have, because we can share with others to show God's love.

Israeli Vegetable Stew

Ingredients

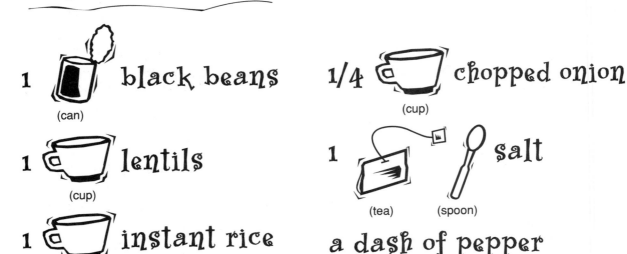

1 (can) black beans

1 (cup) lentils

1 (cup) instant rice

2 (table) (spoon) -s oil

1/4 (cup) chopped onion

1 (tea) (spoon) salt

a dash of pepper

8 (cup) -s water

Cooking Instructions

Place the beans, lentils, rice, oil, chopped onion, salt, and pepper in an electric skillet at low heat or Crock-Pot set on high. Add the water. Cook for 20 to 30 minutes. Stir occasionally.

Rhoda: God's Pray-and-Tell Servant

Kids Can tell others about answered prayer.

Your Kids and the Bible

Rhoda's story provides a wonderful example of a child who took prayer seriously and who told others when she saw God answered her prayers. As a servant girl in a Christian home, Rhoda had responsibilities in serving the family. But in many Christian homes, servants were almost like members of the family. Rhoda appears to have been part of the prayer meeting being held in the home where she lived.

The Christians who were gathered that evening knew what had already happened: Herod, angry at the Christians, had begun causing trouble for people who believed in Jesus. He had discovered that the Jews were pleased when he persecuted Christians, so he carried out the execution of James, one of Jesus' disciples. Now Herod had imprisoned Peter, and the Christians figured it was just a matter of time until Herod executed him as well. They were praying for Peter's release (Acts 12:5), but it is likely that they were all wondering if one of them was next in line to be imprisoned or executed.

So when the knock came at the gate in the middle of the night, it probably struck fear in all of them. Maybe Herod's soldiers had come for them. Not wanting to arouse suspicion, they sent Rhoda to answer the knock, as it probably would have been one of her normal duties. Even though the Christians were there to pray, they couldn't believe their ears when Rhoda returned and joyously announced an answer to their prayers: Peter was at the gate. Even the Christians' suggestion that Rhoda was crazy didn't deter this young girl—she insisted that Peter was there. She knew that prayers had been answered, and eventually everyone else saw that she was right.

Even those of us who truly believe in prayer can get so caught up in logic, skepticism, or even the act of praying itself that we don't see when our prayers have been answered. Sometimes it takes a child to point out the obvious—that God has answered. Your kids may be just the discerning ones God can use to make a difference in the lives of those around them.

Simple Supplies

- a bowl or bag of goodies
- cleaning supplies
- a Bible
- paper and pencils
- chalkboard and chalk or newsprint and markers

focus FUN

(5 minutes)

Somewhere in the room, hide a bowl or bag of goodies. Make it difficult enough to find that kids won't see it without really looking through things.

When class begins, say: **Somewhere in this room, I've hidden some goodies. In a moment, I'm going to let you look for them. Whoever finds them may take one, but that person must also let the others know where the goodies are.** Send the kids to search. After the snacks are found and everyone has one, ask:

- **When the goodies were discovered, how did everyone else find out about them?**
- **How would you have responded if you had been the one who found them?**
- **How do people usually respond when they discover good things?**

Say: **In today's lesson, we're going to learn about a girl in the Bible who discovered a good thing—an answer to prayer—and we're going to see how excited she was to tell others about it, too!**

A Walk in Rhoda's Shoes

(10 minutes)

Before class, arrange several different ways children can serve in the classroom, such as washing windows, washing a chalkboard, emptying trash, or straightening up bookshelves. If you want to really make the point, find dirty places around the church that kids can clean. Say: **The girl we're studying today was a servant girl. Right now we're going to experience what it's like to be servants.** Give each child one or two of the tasks you've arranged in advance. Assign tasks according to the abilities of your kids at their ages. While kids are doing their tasks, be strict with them. Don't allow any talking or horseplay. Require them to do their tasks well.

After the kids have finished, ask:

- **How do you think this activity was like being a servant in Bible times?**
- **How was it different?**
- **What would it be like to have to do those kinds of tasks all day long?**

Say: **Rhoda was a servant girl in a Christian household. She probably was treated with respect, but many servants in that day were treated very poorly. Some were slaves who had to work for little or no pay. Rhoda was probably happy to be serving in a Christian home.** Ask:

● **How do you think serving in a Christian home would be different from serving in a non-Christian home?**

● **How easy would it be to be joyful as a servant?**

● **How would being a Christian be a help to a servant?**

At this point, you may want to share some of the information from the "Your Kids and the Bible" section of this lesson (p. 77). Then say: **Rhoda was a faithful servant who served God as she was serving the family she worked for. And today's story will show us how she helped others recognize an answer to prayer.**

(20 minutes)

A Leap into the Bible

Have kids number off by threes. Say: **As I read this story, I want each of you to pretend you're one of the people in the story. Every so often I will stop reading and ask you some questions about how you would be feeling as one of those people. Ones, you will be Peter. Twos, you will be Rhoda. Threes, you will be the people praying at Mary's house. Listen carefully as I read, and be ready to answer when I ask you the questions.**

Read aloud Acts 12:1-16: **"It was about this time that King Herod arrested some who belonged to the church, intending to persecute them. He had James, the brother of John, put to death with the sword. When he saw that this pleased the Jews, he proceeded to seize Peter also. This happened during the Feast of Unleavened Bread. After arresting him, he put him in prison, handing him over to be guarded by four squads of four soldiers each. Herod intended to bring him out for public trial after the Passover."**

Ask:

● **How would you be feeling if you were Peter?**

Continue reading: **"So Peter was kept in prison, but the church was earnestly praying to God for him."**

Ask:

● **How would you be feeling if you were the people praying?**

Continue reading: **"The night before Herod was to bring him to trial, Peter was sleeping between two soldiers, bound with two chains, and sentries stood guard at the entrance. Suddenly an angel of the Lord appeared and a light shone in the cell. He struck Peter on the side and woke him up. 'Quick, get up!' he said, and the chains fell off Peter's wrists.**

"Then the angel said to him, 'Put on your clothes and sandals.' And Peter did so. 'Wrap your cloak around you and follow me,' the angel told

him. Peter followed him out of the prison, but he had no idea that what the angel was doing was really happening; he thought he was seeing a vision. They passed the first and second guards and came to the iron gate leading to the city. It opened for them by itself, and they went through it. When they had walked the length of one street, suddenly the angel left him.

"Then Peter came to himself and said, 'Now I know without a doubt that the Lord sent his angel and rescued me from Herod's clutches and from everything the Jewish people were anticipating.' "

Ask:
● How would you be feeling if you were Peter?
● How do you think the people who were praying were feeling at that time of night?
● How do you think Rhoda was feeling?

Continue reading: "When this had dawned on him, he went to the house of Mary the mother of John, also called Mark, where many people had gathered and were praying. Peter knocked at the outer entrance, and a servant girl named Rhoda came to answer the door. When she recognized Peter's voice, she was so overjoyed she ran back without opening it and exclaimed, 'Peter is at the door!' "

Ask:
● What does the story say about how Rhoda was feeling?

Read: " 'You're out of your mind,' they told her. When she kept insisting that it was so, they said, 'It must be his angel.' "

Ask:
● How do you think Rhoda was feeling now?
● How was Peter feeling by this time?
● What were the people in the house feeling?

Read Acts 12:16: "But Peter kept on knocking, and when they opened the door and saw him, they were astonished."

Ask:
● How do you think the people in the house felt then?
● How did Rhoda feel?
● How did Peter feel?

After asking all these questions, have kids form groups with one Peter, one Rhoda, and one praying Christian in each group. Have the group discuss these questions:
● What effect did Rhoda's joyful announcement of answered prayer have at first?
● What might have happened if Rhoda had not insisted she was right?
● How did Rhoda serve God that night?

Have the groups report on what they discussed. Then say: **Rhoda did her part in serving God by joyously pointing out a huge answer to prayer. It was so important to her to tell the others about their answered prayer that she forgot about Peter and left him standing at the gate! We can help** others see answers to prayer, just as Rhoda did.

(15 minutes)

racing AHEAD

Say: **Rhoda saw what God had done in answer to prayer and told others about it. We can do that too.**

Have kids form groups of about four. Be sure there is a child who can write well in each group. Give each group a sheet of paper and a pencil. Have groups brainstorm a list of things they've heard people pray about in the last few weeks. Have them list those prayers on the left side of their papers. If they have trouble thinking of things, prompt them by telling them things people in your church or community have been praying about.

After groups have listed several prayer concerns on their papers, say: **Now we're going to do one more thing with this list. Look at the prayer concerns, and next to each one, write how God has answered that prayer. If nothing has happened, write that. If something has happened, describe it. If something big has happened, be sure to make a special note of it.**

Give kids about five minutes to discuss their lists; then have groups share times they've recognized God's answer to prayers. If the subject of unanswered prayers comes up, you may want to respond by telling kids that sometimes God answers "no" or "wait." We can be sure that God always does what is best for us, even if it doesn't seem like it at the time.

After kids have shared, ask:

● **Do the people you have heard praying about these things on your lists seem to realize how God has answered their prayers? Explain.**

● **How could you help these people think about God's answers to their prayers?** List these ideas on newsprint so you can refer back to them later.

● **What do you think are some of the reasons we sometimes don't recognize answers to our prayers?**

Say: **God used a young girl, Rhoda, to help some very mature Christians recognize that their prayer was being answered. God can use kids like you in the same way he used Rhoda. And we can bring joy to people as Rhoda did when they realize that God is working in their lives.**

following the footsteps

(15 minutes)

Say: **Sometimes we pray about things, and it seems as if nothing happens. But God always knows what's best. He answered the prayers of the early Christians when they prayed for Peter, and Rhoda told them about it. Rhoda's example can**

teacher TIP:

It's likely that at least one of your children has been affected by a story similar to the story of Joshua, Nathan, and Rachel's grandfather and may have an emotional response to open discussion of Grandpa's alcoholism. This is a wonderful opportunity to have a child privately share concerns with you so that you can pray together. Be sure to carefully guard your students' trust in you and to respect their need for confidentiality.

help us remember to pray about things that are important to us and to watch carefully for God's answers. When we recognize God's answers, we can have the joy of sharing them with others. Listen to this true story that happened to three children just like you.

Joshua, Nathan, and Rachel are three real children who prayed earnestly for their grandpa. Their grandpa was an alcoholic and didn't know Jesus. Because of his drinking, Grandpa had sometimes made life difficult for their mother as she grew up. He often became mean and nasty when he was drinking, and he used up a lot of the family's money. Many times he tried to stop drinking, but he just couldn't do it on his own.

Joshua, Nathan, and Rachel prayed that Grandpa would stop drinking, but even more, they prayed that he would come to know Jesus. Months went by, then years. Almost every night the children prayed, but Grandpa never seemed to get better. In fact, he got worse. Eventually, he got very sick, and no one knew how long he would live.

One day, an old, trusted friend visited Grandpa and talked with him about Jesus. Grandpa had heard about Jesus many times throughout his life but never had been ready to really trust him with his life. That day, with his old friend at his side, Grandpa decided to trust Jesus with his whole life. Before the next morning came, Grandpa had gone to be with Jesus in heaven. It had taken a long time, but God answered the prayers of Joshua, Nathan, and Rachel at just the right time. And the three children had the joy of telling everyone that God had answered their prayers.

Ask:

● What are some prayers you've prayed more than once?

● What does the story you just heard remind you to do or not do?

Say: **God listens and answers our prayers. Just as Rhoda and the children we heard about did, we can pray for others and we can keep watching for God's answer. When we do that, we'll be following God and serving him as we serve others.**

Have children think back to their list of suggestions for ways to tell others about answers to prayer. Encourage each child to pick one to do today. Then close the lesson with prayer, asking God to help children tell him about things that concern them and to joyfully tell others when their prayers are answered.

Paul's Nephew: Speaking Up to Protect Others

Kids Can recognize danger and take action to get help.

Your Kids and the Bible

Imagine the story of conspiracy and intrigue in Acts 23:12-22 as a blockbuster hit on the big screen. A boy who has known his incarcerated uncle only through rumor overhears a group of teachers plotting his assassination. The boy, perhaps unbeknown to his mother, claims his right of family visitation at the prison gate and is admitted to see the prisoner. Once there, he explains to his uncle in hushed tones that he has overheard the bizarre plot to take his uncle's life. He knows exactly how and exactly when this mob murder is to occur only by virtue of having been in the right place at the right time. Now, it's up to the boy to expose the conspiracy and save his uncle's life. But what if he is discovered to be the snitch? What will happen to him?

Most of what we believe about Paul's nephew is based on extrapolation. Paul's family is specifically mentioned only in this brief passage. The nephew is the son of Paul's sister. It is believed that Paul's family disowned him when he became a Christian. The members of Paul's family must have continued to live much as they had as he was growing up: emphasizing strict education in and adherence to the laws of the Jews, yet remaining Roman citizens. It is this Roman citizenship that allowed Paul's nephew to effectively act as a double agent—Jewish schoolboy by day and Roman informant by night.

We don't know his exact age. He is described as young, and when he met the

Roman commander, the commander took him by the hand as one would comfort a frightened child.

Based on the word of this young man, Paul was spirited away to safety in Caesarea. We can only guess at the courage required for this boy to tell what his countrymen planned to do. How do this young man's actions apply to kids today? Kids are constantly under pressure to hide information. Learning to keep confidences is an important skill. But learning when to break a confidence to protect someone is just as important.

The character trait required to do this is discernment. Discernment is needed to face many challenges in life, and in this lesson, your kids will explore how they can grow in their ability to discern and develop the courage to act on their convictions in the same brave way Paul's nephew did.

Simple Supplies

- several rolls of masking tape
- newsprint and markers
- small balloons (two per child, plus some extras for emergencies)
- dark construction paper
- a drawing compass, scissors, and a flexible tape measure
- clear tape
- graham crackers and honey
- drinking straws

focus FUN (10 minutes)

Use masking tape to mark a line across the floor of your room. Put another piece of tape across the center of the first piece. Say: **I'm going to read a situation. If you would tell someone about the situation, I want you to stand on the right side of the tape. If you wouldn't tell anyone, stand on the left side of the tape. If you honestly don't know what you would do, stand near the piece of tape at the center.**

Read the following situations, and have kids move to the place they choose. After each situation, ask:

Situation 1

You and your friend are shopping. Your friend's mother takes something from one of the racks and stuffs it inside her purse while you and your friend stand in front of her.

Situation 2

The meanest kid in the school knocks down your little sister. She's not really hurt, but it makes you really mad. When you confront the bully, she tells you if you mess with her, you'll be on the ground, too, and next time she won't be so gentle.

Situation 3

Your town has made it a law that all kids who ride bicycles or tricycles have to wear helmets. Your neighbor kids have helmets, but they never wear them, and their parents don't seem to care.

Situation 4

You're playing outside, and you hear a group of neighbors talking. You know you're not supposed to hear what they are saying because they are whispering. But you hear that they are planning to turn another neighbor's dog loose into the traffic because they are tired of hearing it bark.

● What is the main reason you chose to stand where you are standing?

● What do you think might be the consequence of your choice?

● What do you think might happen if you made the opposite choice?

After you've discussed the children's answers, ask:

● Which situation was the hardest for you to make a choice about? Why?

● Do you think it would be harder to tell on other kids or on adults? Why?

Say: **A young man in the Bible had a difficult thing to do. He had to tell on some people who he had to continue to get along with—some of them were probably his teachers. What are some of the questions you think he had to answer in his own mind before he decided what to do?**

List children's questions on newsprint or a chalkboard so that you can refer to them later during the lesson.

A Walk in Paul's Nephew's Shoes

(25 minutes)

Say: **The boy we are going to learn about is not named in the Bible. All we know is that he was the Apostle Paul's sister's son. That would make him Paul's nephew. We do think that he was a student at the Temple, where he learned the things that all young Jewish boys were expected to learn. As they went to school, they wore special hats called yarmulkes** (YAH-ma-kuhs). **Today we are going to make some yarmulkes to wear.**

Give each child a small balloon to inflate. Have kids use a flexible tape measure to measure around the balloon about one-third of the way from the top. Have each student use a drawing compass to make a circle on dark construction paper as wide across as the distance he or she just measured. Have students cut the circles out and fold them in half, then in quarters, then in eighths. Have each student cut out the eight triangles that are formed by the folds and set them aside.

Show kids how to wrap masking tape around their balloons at the place they measured, sticky side facing out. Have each student add four strips of masking tape over the top of the balloon, attaching these strips to the first strip on each side (see diagram on page 87). Then show kids how to place the construction paper triangles across the tape with the points at the top of the balloons and the bottoms of the triangles stuck to the tape that goes around the balloons. When the children have attached all the triangles, they may tape the outer edges together with clear tape. Then they can remove the balloons, and they will have yarmulkes. They may trim the bottom edges with scissors if they wish.

After the children have made their yarmulkes, encourage them to wear them on the backs of their heads. Say:

In Paul's nephew's school, children may have been given a slate with a passage of Scripture written on it. The teacher would spread honey over the slate, and the children would use pens to trace the words of Scripture, licking their pens between letters. This way the children were "absorbing the Scriptures." To help you get an idea of what that might have been like, we're going to do a short lesson together.

Give each child a drinking straw and a graham cracker spread with a thin layer of honey. Tell kids not to eat the treat, but to do each thing you tell them to do.

teacher TIP:

If you don't have several compasses, consider using string to make a circle. Tie a piece of string to a pencil, and cut it half the length of the child's measurement of the balloon. Then have one child hold the string against the construction paper while another one pulls the string taut and draws the circle with the pencil.

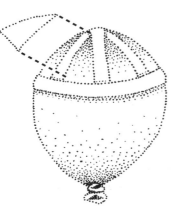

Say: **I'll ask you a question, and you can use your straw to write the answer on your graham cracker. Each time you write an answer, you may lick your straw to taste how sweet the knowledge of the Lord is.**

Ask:

● **Who created the heavens and the earth?**

● **How many commandments are there?**

● **How many Gods are there?**

When children have finished, they may eat their "slates." Say: **The answer to all those questions are found in the Old Testament of the Bible. Those are the Scriptures that Paul's nephew learned, because the books of the New Testament hadn't been written yet. Do you think Paul's nephew had any idea that some day his story would be told in the Scriptures? I think one of the reasons his story is in the Bible is that he had learned so much about right and wrong from the Scriptures. He knew when something was wrong, and he made the choice to get help to protect someone. Let's find out exactly what his story was.**

(10 minutes)

A Leap into the Bible

Have the kids form two groups and sit in lines against opposing walls. Say: **As I tell you this Bible story, which is told in Acts 23:12-22, I want you to listen for several key words. When you hear the word "plot," put your finger up to your lips and say "Shh!" When you hear me say "Christian," clap your hands once and point straight up and say, "He's alive!" When you hear me say, "Paul's nephew," if you're sitting on the right side of the room, say, "Gotta tell, gotta tell, someone is in danger!" Then if you're sitting on the left side of the room, say, "Can't tell, can't tell, these people are your neighbors!"** Practice the cue words with the kids several times, and then begin to tell the story.

When Paul became a Christian (pause), **his family was disgusted. They had raised him to be a good Jew, and in their eyes, believing that Jesus was the Messiah was wrong. Better their son should be dead than to be a Christian!** Pause. **So they probably just acted as though he was dead because the Bible tells us Paul gave up everything to be a Christian.** Pause.

Paul's teaching caused lots of strong feelings among the Jews, so strong that he had to be put in prison just to protect him from being torn to pieces. But in spite of all the chaos, things went on pretty much as usual—at least for Paul's nephew. Pause. **No holidays for him. He probably still had to go to school. No doubt, that's where he learned of the plot.** Pause.

The plot (pause) involved a quiet plan that more than forty men had chosen to participate in. They swore they would not eat until Paul was dead. Now Paul's nephew knew about it. Pause. What would he do about this evil plot (pause), planned all because his uncle was a Christian? Pause. On one hand, his uncle had been disowned. He really wasn't even one of the family anymore. On the other hand, the people in the Temple were planning to break one of the commandments they themselves had taught him. Should he keep the secret of the plot (pause), or should Paul's nephew tell? Pause.

Quickly, he ran to the barracks where Paul was being held. "Uncle," he said, "I've learned of a wicked plot" (pause) "to kill you!" Paul immediately called the guard who came to get Paul's nephew. Pause. Now what was going to happen? This was getting out of hand. The guard was hauling him off to see the man in charge of the whole military force! What should he do? Would they lock him up? Would they lock his friends and neighbors up? All these thoughts and more must have gone through Paul's nephew's mind. Pause. By the time he got to see the man in charge, he must have been as white as a sheet because the official took him by the hand and asked, "What is it you want to tell me?"

One last chance to change his mind. What would Paul's nephew (pause) do? Quickly, he explained the plot. Pause. The official warned him not to tell anyone else what he had revealed. Under armed guard, Paul was whisked away to a place he would be safe for the time being. Once again, Paul was able to go to another city and tell people about being a Christian. Pause.

Ask:

● Have you ever had a real-life struggle about whether to tell on someone?

● How did you decide what to do?

● Which of the questions we wrote earlier on the newsprint might be the most helpful to you?

Say: **Let's see if we can develop a plan of action that might help us in the future.**

 (10 minutes)

 In this activity, kids will develop a flowchart to help them each make a decision about whether to tell on a friend.

Use a piece of newsprint and a marker to draw as you explain. Use the diagram (p. 89) as a model for your discussion. Say: **One way to help us make good choices is to have a plan. This kind of plan is called a flowchart. It helps us see what might happen if we**

make different choices. We can start with a picture of a square. Inside the square, there is a question such as "Is someone doing something I don't like?" If the answer is yes, we draw a line to another square and ask another question. If the answer is no, we don't need to go any further with the flowchart. We can just make a stop sign. Explain a few more steps, then have the kids form mixed age groups. Make sure there is a writer in each group. Give each group a sheet of newsprint and several markers so kids can add colors. If your students are young, you may choose to continue this activity as a whole class, having kids tell you their ideas while you act as their scribe. Kids may use the questions they listed earlier and recorded on newsprint, or they may make up new questions as they go. Be sure to guide kids through the filters of what Scripture says and what God says to them as they pray for his direction, if they don't think of those things on their own.

This activity doesn't have to look perfect or follow a specific formula. Even young children can be coached to think through their decisions in one or two steps. This picture representation can help them remember. In general, the younger the group, the fewer the questions since young children tend to be very "either/or" in their thinking. Older elementary students can grasp more steps. Even if you are not entirely comfortable with this process, it can be very effective for some students' learning styles. You might even consider cutting construction paper shapes and letting the kids write their questions and answers on the shapes. Then kids can move the shapes around to explore different outcomes.

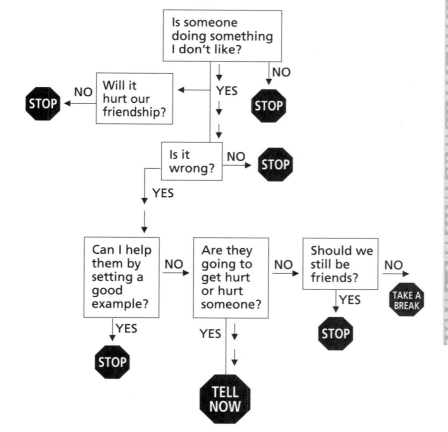

following the footsteps

(5 minutes)

Give kids each another balloon. Have them inflate the balloons and tie them. Ask:

● **If I asked you to squeeze your balloon in your bare hands until it pops how would that make you feel?**

● **What are some concerns you might have?**

● **How are those concerns like or unlike the feeling you might have if you felt that you had to tell on a friend in order to send out a warning?**

Read Psalm 118:6 aloud.

Say: **Close your eyes, and squeeze that balloon until it pops!**

After the kids have broken the balloons, ask:

● **Which of your concerns turned out to be as bad as you thought they might be?**

● **How is being afraid of popping a balloon like being afraid of getting help for someone who may be in danger?**

Say: **Tattling is like breaking a balloon just to make all these little pieces. It is destructive and wrong. But if we are telling to sound a warning for someone who might be in trouble, we can count on the Lord to be with us and protect us, even though we may feel uncomfortable or scared. The Lord was with Paul's nephew when he made the hard choice to tell on his teachers. Because of his nephew's courage to act when he knew there was trouble, Paul's ministry continued. This boy's story can help us remember that we can recognize danger and take action to get help.**

Timothy: An Example at Any Age

Kids Can be an example to all believers.

Your Kids and the Bible

Timothy was a Jewish Greek raised in Lystra in Asia Minor by his Jewish mother, Eunice, and his grandmother Lois, both of whom had become followers of Christ. They made sure Timothy knew God's Word from an early age (Acts 16:1-2; 2 Timothy 1:5). Timothy's father is only briefly mentioned as a Greek. It is believed that his father wasn't living.

We aren't really sure how old Timothy was when he came to know Christ, but it was probably during Paul's first missionary journey to Lystra. Paul heard good things about this young disciple and invited him along on the second missionary journey. This began a mentoring relationship that was unparalleled in Paul's ministry. Paul stepped into the missing father's role in Timothy's life, encouraging him, training him, and being a loving example to him. Timothy in turn became a trusted member of Paul's ministry team and acted on Paul's behalf in many situations.

Timothy's household was a lot like many of today's households in which children are being raised by a single parent in a multicultural environment. Several passages of Scripture indicate that Timothy had some obstacles to overcome, including a natural timidity and sensitivity concerning his youth. Timothy's story offers hope that kids whose home lives are less than perfect can turn out to be outstanding examples of the faithfulness of a loving God. The investment of wise and caring adults can make all the difference. In spite of his youthfulness, Timothy's ministry was significant in several early church congregations. Through his story, your kids can be confident that they can make outstanding contributions to their own church when their speech and lives exemplify love, faith, and purity (1 Timothy 4:12).

Simple Supplies

- one aluminum can for every two children
- bay leaves (two to five per child)
- green construction paper, cut into 1½-inch strips

- tape or stapler
- gold coins or gold wrapping paper
- envelopes
- aluminum foil

focus FUN (10 minutes)

Have children form pairs as they enter the classroom. When all the children have arrived, have each pair decide who will be a Learner and who will be a Mentor. Say: **Now that you've decided who's who, I will tell you that a mentor is someone who has experience doing something. This person is willing to share what he or she knows with someone who is new to that experience. I would like all the Mentors to come and see me privately, while the rest of you turn around and together count aloud as high as you can.**

Show the Mentors how to gently kick an aluminum can so that it goes no farther than about one foot. Tell them that their goal will be to alternate turns kicking their cans with their Learners until they get the cans to the other side of the room, never allowing the cans to go more than a foot at a time. If a Learner kicks it harder or farther than the maximum distance, the Learner and Mentor both will go back to the beginning and start again. Let each Mentor practice this controlled movement one or two times; then have them pick up the cans and stand against a designated wall while you go to count with the other group. Wind up the counting when you see all the Mentors in position.

Say: **The Mentors have learned a skill that they would like to model for you. You will have to watch your Mentor carefully because he or she can only show you what to do, not tell you. Mentors, remember there is to be no talking. This is not a race; it's a skill activity. Learners, join your Mentors and begin.**

> ### teacher TIP:
>
> Have children count in order to prevent them from overhearing or seeing what the other group is doing. If you have another way to separate your two groups, such as sending one group from the room with an assistant, feel free to do that instead.

When all the kids have successfully completed their task, ask:

● **Learners, how would you describe in words what you just did?**

● **How do you think you could teach someone else what you just learned?**

● **Mentors, what was it like to try to teach in the way you did?**

● **What would have made your job easier?**

Say: **The relationship you just experienced was a little like Paul's relationship with a young man by the name of Timothy. In the same way that I showed and told the Mentors what to teach so that they could show the Learners, Paul showed Timothy how to live and asked Timothy to go and show others, even though he was much younger than many other Christians. Timothy's life helps us to know that kids can be an example to all believers.**

A Walk in Timothy's Shoes
(15 minutes)

Say: **Timothy had an interesting background. His mother was Jewish, so according to Jewish laws Timothy was Jewish too. But his father was Greek, and Timothy grew up in a Greek-speaking city. Since the Bible tells us nothing else about his father, many people believe that he may have died when Timothy was quite young.**

Greeks didn't keep the laws of the Old Testament as the Jews did. Even people who had been raised as Jews but had become Christians kept the Jewish law. We know that Timothy's mother, Eunice, and his grandmother Lois taught him the Scripture. But we also know that he didn't keep all the laws as a child. In fact, it's likely that even though he learned the Scriptures from his family, he probably learned other things from Greek culture.

Greek children were taught at the gymnasium. What do children today do at the gymnasium? Pause for students to answer.

Children at Greek gymnasiums did things like that too. But they also learned their regular school subjects there. Greeks made physical education as important as reading and writing. Greek games (which led to the modern Olympics) were originally festivals to honor Greek gods. Ask:

● **How do you think Timothy might have felt about the differences between the Jewish traditions he was taught and the Greek world he lived in?**

● **How do you think Timothy's experiences might have helped him in sharing the good news about Jesus?**

Say: **One way his experiences may have helped him was to give him a special understanding of the challenges of Christian life. In one of the teaching letters Paul sent to Timothy, he compared the life of faith to the fights of the Greek games. In these games, the winner was given a crown** of laurel or olive leaves. We're going to make a crown to use later in our lesson.

Show kids how to make a crown with the construction paper strips. Have them help one another staple or tape the crowns so that the crowns fit snugly. Then hand several bay leaves to each child. Say: **Paul's main message to Timothy was to live as an example of faith, even though he was young. Each of us can be an example to those around us. In a minute, I'm going to ask you to give your laurel leaves away to help you realize you are always an example. Give one of your leaves to someone and tell how you have noticed him or her being an example of faithful living.**

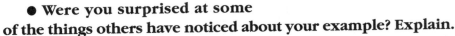

After the children have given away their leaves, ask:

● **Were you surprised at some of the things others have noticed about your example? Explain.**

● **Who are some of the people who have set an example that you feel good about following?**

● **Who are some people you want to set an example for?**

Say: **Smell the leaves you are holding. These bay leaves come from the laurel tree. They have a very strong smell. Timothy needed to be strong to do all that God had planned for him, just as you need to be strong to set a good example to others. Tape or glue the leaves to your crown, and put the crown aside while we learn a little more about the people Paul asked Timothy to be an example to, and exactly what Paul encouraged him to do.**

A Leap into the Bible

(15 minutes)

Choose four locations around the room or church. In the first area, you won't need any supplies. In the second area, place the gold items. In the third area, place the envelopes. In the fourth area, place the aluminum foil.

Say: **We're about to take a trip around Greece, Macedonia, and Asia Minor to some churches Timothy ministered to. Timothy went with Paul on several missionary journeys, but perhaps the most important thing he did was to go into places that Paul for some reason could not visit.**

Lead the children in an imaginary climb up a mountain. Say: **High on a hill stood the big city of Corinth. Corinth was an important city to the Romans. It had been rebuilt and was a beautiful city in the days of Timothy's ministry there. The message to the church at Corinth was to live upright lives. Stand up really straight and tall to remind you of the** upright life Timothy needed to show the Corinthians.

Later Timothy was sent to Philippi. Lead children to the next area. **At one time, Philippi was a gold-mining area. Take one of these gold items to remind you of Philippi, another Roman city. Paul sent Timothy there to look after the Philippians. Make binoculars with your hands, and look around. Paul said he knew Timothy would look out for Jesus' interests in Philippi rather than his own selfish interests. That's how Paul hoped the Philippians would choose to live, too.**

Walk to the next station. Just before you get there, change your movements to swimming motions. Say: **The city of Thessalonica was a seaport city. When the Christians there were having trouble, Paul sent Timothy to be an encouragement to them. He also wanted a report back about how they were doing. Take an envelope to remind you that Timothy was a messenger for Paul at Thessalonica and in other cities.**

"Swim" out of Thessalonica and on to Ephesus. Give each child a small scrap of aluminum foil. Say: **When Paul first went to the impressive city of Ephesus, he reached so many people with the good news of Jesus that the silversmiths who made statues for the worship of the goddess Diana became angry because they thought their business of goddess-making was over! They chased Paul out of town. Ephesus was the city that Timothy stayed in the longest. Timothy received letters there from Paul that encouraged him in all the skills he needed to be a pastor for this church. He told Timothy, "Don't let anyone look down on you because you are young, but set an example for the believers in speech, in life, in love, in faith and in purity... Be diligent in these matters; give yourself wholly to them so that everyone may see your progress"** (1 Timothy 4:12 and 15).

Paul's letters to Timothy asked him to always be looking at himself to make sure the example he was setting was good. Look into the piece of aluminum foil at your reflection. Ask yourself this question, but don't answer it out loud: If Paul were talking to me about being an example, what kind of example would I look like? Encourage the children to be completely quiet for about thirty seconds as they consider this question.

Say: **Timothy was also with Paul and was Paul's scribe as Paul dictated letters to other churches. He watched Paul closely and followed him as Paul followed Jesus.** Ask:

● **Why was Paul able to be such a good example to Timothy?**

● **Where did Paul get his ideas about how Timothy should behave?**

● **Where can we get the best ideas for how we should live to set a good example?**

● **Why is it important to set a good example no matter how old we are?**

Say: **Just as Timothy was sent to different places to be an example to the believers, Jesus wants us to be an example to the believers wherever we go.**

racing AHEAD

(15 minutes)

Form four groups. Give the first group a piece of paper that says, "in speech"; give group two a piece of paper that says, "in love"; give group three one that says, "in faith"; and give group four one that says, "in purity."

Have each group appoint a Detective, a Scribe, and an Attorney. The Detective will seek evidence from each person in the group, the Scribe will record the findings, and the Attorney will report the findings to the whole group. Say: **According to the Bible, it is important to set an example in each of these areas. Your job as a defense team is to tell why your area is the most important of all four. To support your argument, list the three best ways to set an example in your area.** You may wish to post all four areas on newsprint or on a chalkboard to help kids remember what other groups are defending.

Give the groups five minutes to create their cases; then have them give their reports to the whole group. After all the teams have reported, say: **You have all presented terrific evidence. Now each of you becomes a member of the jury to decide which is most important for *your* life this week. There are no right or wrong verdicts, just important opportunities, because kids really can be an example to all believers.**

following the footsteps

(5 minutes)

Have children hold the crowns they constructed earlier and sit face to face with a partner. When all the children are seated, say: **Think about your verdict in the last activity. Share with your partner what you decided was important to try to do in your life and why you made that decision.**

Give kids about one minute to share. Then say: **I'd like you to pray for each other to be "winners" this week in that particular way. When you have finished praying for your partner, place the victor's crown on his or her head and remind your partner to depend on God's help to be an example to believers by the way he or she lives.**

Give kids about two minutes to complete your instructions; then close with this prayer: **Dear God, thank you for each of these kids. We know you are trusting us to be examples in speech, in life, in love, in faith, and in purity, no matter how young or old we are. Help each of us to be winners in our goals this week. In Jesus' name, amen.**